The Behaviour Management Toolkit

The Behaviour Management Toolkit

Avoiding Exclusion at School

Chris Parry-Mitchell

Los Angeles | London | New Delhi
Singapore | Washington DC

SAGE Publications Ltd
1 Oliver's Yard
55 City Road
London EC1Y 1SP

SAGE Publications Inc.
2455 Teller Road
Thousand Oaks, California 91320

SAGE Publications India Pvt Ltd
B 1/I 1 Mohan Cooperative Industrial Area
Mathura Road
New Delhi 110 044

SAGE Publications Asia-Pacific Pte Ltd
3 Church Street
#10–04 Samsung Hub
Singapore 049483

Library of Congress Control Number: 2011938139

British Library Cataloguing in Publication data

A catalogue record for this book is available from the British Library

ISBN 978-1-4462-1074-1
ISBN 978-1-4462-1075-8 (pbk)

Typeset by C&M Digitals (P) Ltd, Chennai, India
Printed in India at Replika Press Pvt Ltd
Printed on paper from sustainable resources

Contents

CD table of contents

Session 1

Session 2

Session 3

Session 4

Session 5

Session 6

Session 7

Session 8

Session 9

Session 10

Appendices

About the author

Chris Parry-Mitchell is a teacher and head of department with over 20 years of experience working in a wide range of educational settings. She is an INLPTA International NLP Trainers Association Master Practitioner of NLP. Chris is Principal Trainer for Education at the Instit2te of NLP for public service as well as working for one of the major examination boards delivering training on effective teaching strategies. Her passion is not just about teaching a subject but also about enabling and assisting young people to understand how they and others operate and to achieve success. This passion led her to devise and run the 'Know How Programme' which this book is based on. It runs in Preston for those young people who are at risk or not thriving within their educational setting. Chris has strong values about fairness and opportunity and believes that most young people are doing the best they can with what they know at that moment and, given better strategies, will behave and perform differently.

For training purposes, Chris' contact details are provided below:
E-mail: c.mitchell_@hotmail.co.uk
Tel: 07773 937512

Acknowledgements

I am sincerely grateful to the young people of Preston who in the last four years have helped create this programme with their honesty, trust in me and belief that things can be different, despite in some instances the odds being very much stacked against them. Their enthusiasm coupled with my belief that things have to be fair has made me passionate about working with young people and their families, whatever their backgrounds.

My very special thanks go to Chris and Glenda Grimsley of the Instit2te of NLP for public service. They are expert trainers and have guided me with their knowledge and friendship. This book would not have happened without their support and thus I am grateful to them.

I am also very grateful to Andrew Swift (Swifty) my Higher Level Teaching Assistant who has worked with me in successfully delivering this programme to over 250 young people; his values, expertise, enthusiasm and talent for acting have been much appreciated!

Thanks also go to Julie Bather, Headteacher at Larches House Short Stay School, Preston, and the Secondary Heads, Preston District Six, for giving me the opportunity to develop and effectively use this work as the Know How Progamme at the Orchard.

Thank you also to Pearson for permission to reprint an image on p.6 from Maslow, A.H. (1987) *Motivation and Personality*, Hong Kong: Longman Asia Ltd.

I would also like to thank the team at Sage, especially Jude Bowen for her guidance and experience and Nicola Marshall for all of her hard work. Thank you also to Stephen Karpman whose feedback and support were much appreciated.

My gratitude also goes to Amanda Moore, Caitlin Walker, Margaret Bamforth and Lisa Robinson for their continued friendship and support – and most importantly to John, Nathan and Ellen for their patience in answering 'Does this make sense?' whilst it has all been put together.

Chris Parry-Mitchell

For Nath and Ells

How to use this book

This book started out as 'The Know How' and came about when I was asked to run an Inclusion Programme for young people who were displaying a variety of behaviours and were just not 'thriving' within their mainstream schools. They came to me one day a week for ten weeks and I had to do something with them that would stop them from being permanently excluded! Using my enthusiasm for working with young people, coupled with my firm belief that they were no different from me on a fundamental human level, I accepted the challenge and put together this programme. This book is for all those people who want to help young people build resilience and succeed.

It illustrates a psycho-educational and metacognitive programme which is aimed at enabling young people by teaching them how to communicate and behave in more useful ways. The programme is based on a range of well-established frameworks and translates some of these into young-people friendly language, activities and techniques.

It is aimed at 10 to 18 year olds and has been rigorously tested and amended by my occasionally reluctant participants but very willing critics. The students I have worked with have had a wide range of concerns from poor motivation, low self-esteem, anger and aggression, to low aspirations, poor attendance and engagement. Some of them have been in mainstream schools and others have already been excluded and have experience of other educational provision. This book is by no means a cure-all and I am sure that in using the content young people will suggest amendments and improvements to the language and examples.

The book can be followed as a ten-week programme of work either with an individual or a group of young people. It can also just as easily be used on a session-by-session basis as and when the need arises, as all of these focus on specific areas or concerns a young person may have and can therefore be used discretely.

Each session includes detailed delivery and guidance notes, photocopiable student worksheets, and a list of the resources required. Timings of tasks and activities are given as an indicator of activity length. For example, 45 minutes is a guideline for the instruction, discussion and completion of a worksheet. This is a flexible timing guide, however, as discussions with young people can be quite abrupt or lengthy depending on the topic! I have highlighted some top tips and common pitfalls, as well as given case studies of how these have been used previously with young people.

The tasks and activities are not gender specific. However, when delivered, alterations in language or the specific examples used may be needed to suit the audience, age range, or needs of the young people involved.

At the root of this programme – which the young people called 'The Know How', as that is what it gives them – are some straightforward beliefs that I hold: I like children and young people but I am not the expert on their worlds. Because of this they can teach me just as much as I can teach them.

Points to consider

Before you embark on using this book there are a number of things that should be considered in order to ensure its success.

- *Size of the group*: as much of the work involves the young people discussing their ideas, and understanding and relating new knowledge to their own lives and experiences, a full assembly room of young people is too many! A group of ten is ideal as this number allows staff involved to monitor and work alongside students as they complete the work.

- In theory, because of the nature of the work, *the group should be closed* with the participants decided at the start: this is especially important if the book is being used as a ten-week programme of work.

- *Stability, safety and consistency are key*: as young people are learning about themselves the same member of staff should deliver the whole programme and boundaries and expectations can then be made clear right from the start.

- *Geography of the group and room layout*: the content is best delivered around a table using a flip chart to explain points. This enables the students to chat and work together with the teacher or facilitator sitting as part of the group. If this book is used in work with individuals then staff should sit alongside each young person as they complete their work.

- *Parental consent may be needed* if the programme is to be run over a course of ten weeks: at the back of this book you will find some examples of possible forms which can be used to decide on participants and inform parents.

- *Have individual folders ready for the students*: using these means they can complete the worksheets and then store them safely.

- In my experience, there are *some common pitfalls to be aware of* when working with young people: their openness and honesty will sometimes catch you unaware. It is therefore recommended that you follow the guidance in Session 3 about establishing the groundrules whether or not you intend to follow the whole programme or bits of it.

- Make it clear to the young people that should information be disclosed which is of concern, you have a *duty of care* to pass it on to the relevant people.

- I have found that if you spend time *establishing a positive rapport* with the young people and don't judge them, they will respond better to the work and content and be more open to you assisting and guiding them. This can be very difficult sometimes, especially when you are faced with challenging behaviour and young people from very vulnerable and diverse settings. Remain calm and consistent and employ humour!

- Young people in their teenage years are often only interested in the opinions of their peer group, with parents and teachers merely becoming background noise. They do, however, respond to shame and a quick wit; use both wisely if these are necessary and appropriate.

1

Introducing the toolkit: establishing a safe group and finding out what the issues are

This session examines how to establish a functioning group and the ground rules which the group will operate under whilst also gaining the students' perspective on any current areas of concern. It also introduces the concept of Maslow's Hierarchy of Needs to students.

The deliberate structuring and forming of the group and the establishment of negotiated ground rules will ensure that the students feel safe and involved and will therefore be able to communicate openly about the behaviours they or others are concerned about.

Worksheet 1.1:   Introducing the group (40 minutes)

Negotiating the ground rules (30 minutes)

Mr Maslow's Triangle: practical task (45 minutes)

Worksheet 1.2:   What's happening now, what do I want and what do I need? (25 minutes)

Worksheet 1.3:   The Circuit of Change (10 minutes)

Timings are a guide for discussions and the completion of the relevant worksheet.

Resources required: photocopies of Worksheets 1.1, 1.2 and 1.3; flip-chart paper; newspapers; magazines; paper; glue; pens; pencils; rulers

Recommended further reading

Maslow, A.H. (1987) *Motivation and Personality,* Hong Kong: Longman Asia Ltd. This can provide more information on the work of Abraham Maslow.

Teacher's notes

Worksheet 1.1: Introducing the group (40minutes)

This worksheet activity formally establishes the group.

It is done to establish a working relationship between group members and staff and also helps to develop rapport between all involved. It allows everyone to learn something about others in the group in a safe environment; this in turn allows the students to feel valued and the group to be formed.

Each student interviews their partners using the questions on the worksheet and notes down the answers.

The students introduce each other by reading out the answers they have written down to the questions; namely, 'This is xxxx, he is 13 years old, his birthday is in March, his favourite food is pizza, his favourite lesson PE and his favourite band xxxx.' Students will then swap over. At the end of each section the students will need to change partners and repeat the process.

Top tips and common pitfalls

Invest time in this worksheet activity and be involved in it. This is important for creating a non-judgemental atmosphere and will pay dividends in establishing rapport and a relationship with the students. Ultimately this means that they will trust you and therefore engage fully in the tasks and you will be able to influence them in the change process they start.

Make sure when partners are changed that all the students are involved.

This can be quite a fun activity, especially if members of staff take part and are honest about their choice of music, for example, which – as it will probably be different from that of the students – will start a bit of friendly banter!

Case study

Students meeting together as a group for the first time will usually begin this activity being very wary of one another – the atmosphere will be like that of a dentist's waiting room. They will know something is going to happen but they won't know whether they will like it. After this task the tension will start to evaporate and friendship and trust will begin to appear.

'Introducing ... '

Name	
Age	
Birthday	
Favourite food	
Favourite lesson	
Favourite band	

'Introducing ... '

Name	
Brothers? Sisters?	
Pets' names?	
Favourite football team?	
Favourite sandwich filling?	
Favourite film?	

'Introducing ... '

Name	
What sort of job would you like to do?	
Have you met anyone famous? Or been on the TV? Or radio?	
What would you like to do if anything were possible? Swimming with dolphins?	
What would be your best present if money were no object?	

Teacher's notes

Negotiating the ground rules (30 minutes)

This is a discussion task to establish the ground rules for the group.

As it is done in a negotiated manner, everyone involved will develop a sense of ownership and belonging. This will also ensure that they begin to develop a group identity.

These ground rules will be written using the 4MAT which was developed by Bernice McCarthy in the late 1970s (www.aboutlearning.com) from the learning cycle put forward by David Kolb (1984). The 4MAT is based on the assumption that as human beings we will have unconscious questions that will need answering so that we can engage, learn and understand. The four questions are 'What?', 'Why?', 'How?' and 'What if?/What next?' Individuals with a 'What' preference will like facts, information and to know what the experts think. Those with a 'Why' preference will need to have personal meaning created for them, namely, 'What is in it for me (WIIFM) for learning or engaging?' Those with a 'How' preference will enjoy applying their learning and those with a 'What if?/What next?' preference will be thinking how they can use and adapt the learning in the future. Education tends to be mainly 'What?' and 'How?' – the passing on of facts and information and how these will be needed in an examination. Young people who have attended our programme have had a mainly 'Why' preference, namely, 'What is in it for me for behaving in this lesson, attending school, learning algebra!'

Using four separate pieces of flip-chart paper note down 'What?' on the first one, 'Why?' on the second, 'How?' on the third, and 'What next?' on the final piece. The 'What' becomes the actual rule stated in the positive, namely, 'All mobile phones on silent whilst the group is working.' The 'Why' is the reason for having the rule, namely 'Because if a phone rings it will disturb the group and it is disrespectful.' The 'How' translates into 'How will we know if this rule has been broken? What will we see and hear?', for example 'it ringing or beeping', and the 'What next?' indicates the consequences the group decides for the behaviour, namely 'one warning and then it gets confiscated until the end of the session.'

The ground rules are then displayed and referred to throughout the programme.

Top tips and common pitfalls

Have an idea of the ground rules you want and guide students here. I have been pleasantly surprised when completing this and most groups will come up with similar rules.

Focusing on 'why' each of the ground rules is needed allows students to be more accepting of them.

You may be surprised at how harsh the consequences they want to impose will be! Use a voting system if there are disagreements here.

Once these two tasks have been completed there will usually be a distinct change of atmosphere, especially if the students do not know each other at the start of the session.

> ## Case study
>
> I have found that the few young people who have broken the ground rules have imme-diately taken the consequences without fuss, even Simon (aged 14) who was on his way to being permanently excluded. Tidying up after the session was the consequence of interrupting others whilst they spoke. The look on the face of a member of staff who visited us to see Simon doing this without a fuss was one of amazement; this member of staff had only ever seen him running around school shouting and swearing at people!

Teacher's notes

Mr Maslow's Triangle: practical activity (45 minutes)

This is a practical task to develop an understanding of Maslow's hierarchy of needs. (Maslow, 1954). Maslow's theory helps us understand how as human beings we are motivated to 'be all we can be' and to self-actualise. The hierarchy suggests that we are motivated to fulfil the needs in order, starting at the base before moving up. As we satisfy the needs in the lower level of the diagram we can then move on to satisfy the needs related to personal development. Maslow believed that the needs were linked to instincts and played a major role in motivating our behaviour. This model allows the students to understand what they need first as individuals in order to survive, feel safe and belong before they can then feel positive about themselves and achieve. It can be also used as a personal 'self-checking' list for when they are feeling less resourceful.

Draw Mr Maslow's Triangle on to a piece of flip-chart paper and ask the students to contribute examples for each section. Students can then create their own triangles on a large piece of paper and cut out examples from newspapers and magazines to fill each of the sections. The finished pieces of work can be displayed afterward.

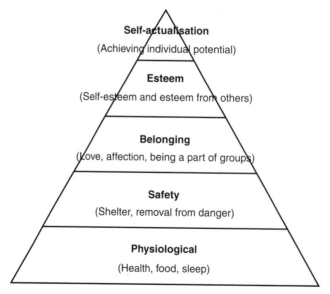

Figure 1.1   Maslow, Abraham, H.; Frager, Robert, D. (Editor); Fadiman, James (Editor), *Motivation and Personality*, 3rd, © 1987. Printed and Electronically reproduced by permission of Pearson Education, Inc., Upper Saddle River, New Jersey.

Top tips and common pitfalls

Whilst the group is working, observe how they are interacting to spot any patterns.

Relate their experience in the group in this first session back to Mr Maslow's Triangle. For example, one of the basic needs, shelter, has been met by the fact that the group are warm and inside in a room; ground rules have been established thereby meeting the need for security and order; and an activity which introduced everyone met the need for a sense of belonging. The work over the coming weeks will therefore look at the top two sections of Mr Maslow's Triangle. This review of their experience will help to reinforce their understanding of the work covered in this task.

Teacher's notes

Worksheet 1.2: What's happening now, what do I want and what do I need? (25 minutes)

This series of worksheets aims to discover what the current areas of concern are from each student's perspective and how they would prefer things to be if a magic wand could be waved.

It enables the students and staff to recognise and gain an insight into the issues that exist and how these are impacting. It also allows students to begin to set out what they ultimately want to achieve and establish as well as what resources they already have and use that could be transferred to their current situation.

The students need to complete the three worksheets in turn, discussing their answers with the group after each one is completed.

Staff can note these down for their records if necessary and they can be referred to over the course of the programme.

Top tips and common pitfalls

When completing these worksheets keep the students focused by not giving them long to complete each one, as otherwise it can become a competition to see whose first worksheet is the worst and they will all begin to associate with and relive the situations.

As they complete the third worksheet guide them into thinking of situations they have behaved and coped well with. For example, do they control their temper when on a sports field? If so, then they already have the resources they need to stay calm. They only need to transfer these to other situations.

Be prepared for their honesty when completing these sheets and do not make judgements.

These tasks can be done in isolation or at the start of a session. It is useful to complete these worksheets at any first meeting with a group or individual as it is a non-judgemental way of gaining insights on students' perspective of their behaviours or situations.

What's happening now, what do I want, and what do I need?

Sometimes other people make comments about our behaviour and sometimes how we behave disappoints us. To change this we need information on three things.

Number 1: What's happening now?

What is happening now for you? What are the problems/issues? When do these problems **not happen** or when do they **happen less?** Think about your behaviours in school and at home that are causing you or others concern and list them below:

-
-
-
-
-
-

Number 2: What do I want?

Thinking about your Number 1 list write down how you would want things to be. Think *'if I had a magic wand how would I change things for the better?'* Remember this is about **you** and **your behaviours** and not about changing other people.

-
-
-
-
-
-

Number 3: What do I need?

Resources: So now you know what the issues are and what you would rather have, for this final part you must think about the things you will need to help you get what you want. Think about all the skills you already have that you could use now to help you, and think about people who may be able to help you or who you need to talk to. Then write these below.

-
-
-
-
-
-

Now what is the first thing **you** are going to do to make things change?

> ## Case study
>
> Isaac (13) completed these sheets with honesty, telling of the situations he found him-self at school and at home. When it came to completing the second sheet, he wrote simply, 'What do I want? I just want to be normal and like everyone else.'

Teacher's notes

Worksheet 1.3: The circuit of change (15 minutes)

The circuit of change is an overview of a process of change and shows how it can be achieved and the route we will usually need to follow when we want to change behaviours.

This worksheet allows the students to see that change is a process that we all go through as human beings. It establishes that it is possible and can be achieved and even if we have a day when we slip back then all is not lost and we can get back on track.

Introduce the worksheet using a story to illustrate how the process works. The students can follow a specimen story on their own worksheets.

The students must mark the current day's date next to the position they think they are at on the circuit of change.

This sheet can be referred to over the course of the programme as required, with the students updating their positions as they make progress.

> ## Top tips and common pitfalls
>
> When giving a specimen story to illustrate the process of change, use one that the students can relate to e.g., someone giving up smoking or losing weight.
>
> Ensure that they are aware that it is normal to end up in the middle of the circuit at some point and that doesn't mean they won't ultimately achieve their goal.

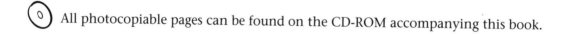 All photocopiable pages can be found on the CD-ROM accompanying this book.

 **CHANGE**

The Circuit of Change

When we change our behaviour we go around the Circuit of Change. It helps us move away from the problems we had and move towards what we want. Follow the numbers around and decide where you are already. Notice that the box in the middle does not have a number because sometime we slip into this box and that is fine. We just have to hop back out and carry on ...

1. What behaviour?: this is where we think '*I don't have a problem, what are they on about?*' and where we don't understand or even see the negatives in our behaviour

6. The End: This is the '*it's sorted*' box. We have changed our behaviour and done it differently for a while. '*Well done!*' '*OK ... What's next?*'

CHANGE

2. Thinking: here we start to wonder about changing ...'*erm OK, maybe*': we might be unsure about how to start

Uh oh! It's happened again: this is when we sometimes slip back in to old behaviours or patterns and it is perfectly normal. '*Ah well! Let's start again*'

3. Get ready: here we know we want to change and we start to think about how we can do this. We can set our goals '*I want ...*'

5. Carry it on: here we can keep our goals in mind, keep encouraging ourselves and remember what is going well: '*I can do this.*'

4. Action: here we can get going with our goals: '*Bring it on ...*'

2

Games, hooks and tactics: common communication scenarios for young people

This session introduces the topic of Transactional Analysis (TA) developed by Eric Berne in the 1950s. TA was devised as a framework for understanding the interactions we have with other people and is therefore useful for young people as it gives an insight into the communications they have with others and explains why that communication sometimes breaks down.

The session starts with a repeated task which allows students to recognise the successes they have had since the last session and they can also discuss aspects of their behaviour which have been less successful. A series of tasks then allows them to explore their interactions using TA. An understanding of these concepts helps students to self-assess their communication with others and this can be used to group-regulate any stories which emerge during the programme where students have behaved less successfully.

Worksheet 2.1:   What has gone well this week? (20 minutes)

Worksheet 2.2:   Analysing our communication (45 minutes)

Worksheet 2.3:   Warm fuzzies and cold pricklies (30 minutes)

Worksheet 2.4:   Hooks and games (30 minutes)

Timings are a guide for discussions and the completion of the relevant worksheet.

Resources required: photocopies of Worksheets 2.1, 2.2, 2.3 and 2.4; flip-chart paper; pens; pencils; rulers; paper; Post-it notes; posters of celebrities

Recommended further reading

Berne, E. (1964) *Games People Play,* New York: Grove Press. Provides information about TA.
Freed, A. and Freed, M. (1971) *TA for Kids,* Rolling Hills Estates, CA: Jalmar Press. This provides a readable introduction to TA for young people.

Steiner, C. (1977) *The Original Warm Fuzzy Tale,* Sacramento, CA: Jalamar Press. The original story of warm fuzzies and cold prickles.

Teacher's notes

Worksheet 2.1: What has gone well this week? (20 minutes)

This worksheet helps to develop an individual's self-esteem and is done on a weekly basis. It enables the students to reflect on what has happened during the past week.

Individuals who have good self-esteem can notice all the small steps that they have made along the way to achieving a goal. However those who have lower self-esteem rather than noting their own progress will tend to constantly compare themselves to a perceived expert and therefore will never feel they have achieved. This task thus begins to reinforce for the students the positive aspects of their behaviour and allows for praise to be received from the group.

The worksheet is completed by the students individually and once this has been done the written contributions for each section will be discussed as a group, starting with the positive aspects. This allows for praise to be received and some discussion and analysis to occur in a safe environment covering the less positive aspects of their week. Completing this task each session with a group ensures that the students are noticing aspects of their life, namely, the small steps, which are going well or are positive and so this helps to develop their self-esteem.

Once discussed, the students must select one example from the top of their worksheet and illustrate it. This is then used on a wallchart with their name attached which follows their progress over the rest of the sessions.

Top tips and common pitfalls

Students are not always good at writing down what has gone well and may need some prompting. I usually give them a few examples verbally of the things they could write down and this seems to encourage them to think of other things. For example, 'arrived at school on time, stayed in lessons, remembered equipment or sports kit'.

Some students for whatever reason will have difficult weeks and when this happens ask them to think of anything that has gone well, from speaking politely to just one person (even if it is you), to making a parent a cup of coffee or keeping their room tidy.

Pay close attention to the students when they are filling in the worksheet so that you can prompt and assist those who may be struggling.

When the students read out their examples to the group remind them of the ground rules and enforce these as necessary.

Praise, clap, cheer as appropriate for all the positive things they note down!

Ask the group for verbal feedback as appropriate on the less positive aspects of the week. Keep the discussion on this part of the worksheet moving so it doesn't become competitive, namely, on whose behaviour has been the worst. The students will attempt to justify their behaviour so keep your feedback to them non-judgemental and evidence-based if possible.

What has gone well this week?

Name:

Thinking about this last week at school and at home list three things that have **'gone well'**.
☺☺☺

Possible ideas: you had a good lesson/day; you completed some work in class; you completed some homework; you spoke politely to people; you have been on time …

1.

2.

3.

Choose your best one from these three and draw it on a piece of paper.

Now write down any things that 'haven't gone as well' this week. ☺☹☺

1.

2.

3.

Teacher's notes

Worksheet 2.2: Analysing our communication: an introduction to Transactional Analysis (45 minutes)

This worksheet introduces the students to the basic concepts of Transactional Analysis developed by Eric Berne in the 1950s. TA is a framework for understanding the interactions an individual has with others, some of which can become repetitive patterns. Berne determined that when communicating with others we can do so from one of three ego states: Parent, Adult or Child. The ego state diagram is drawn as three circles sitting on top of one another with P in the top one, A in the centre one, and C at the bottom. Berne believed that there were three basic facts about people; that at one time all of us will have known someone who acted as a parent, that we were all a child once, and that we can all respond to the here-and-now adult.

Using the ego state model we can examine our interactions with other people. When we have a complementary transaction (e.g., Adult to Adult), namely, 'What time is it?' 'It's five o'clock', then things will go smoothly. However if we have a crossed transaction (e.g., Adult to Parent), namely, A: 'What time is it?' P: 'Why can't you tell the time yourself?', then our communication can break down or leave people feeling uncomfortable. With young people what can happen is that they are spoken to in Adult yet they respond in Child which then encourages a response in Parent and trouble ensues!! For example, 1: In Adult, 'Have you done your homework?' 2: In Child, 'Nah!' 1: In Parent, 'Why do you never do your homework?' 2: In Child, 'Why do you always have a go at me for nothing!', and so on.

Understanding these concepts allows students to see how they play a part in any interaction they have with others. It also allows them to recognise the ego state they and others are communicating from and to change this if necessary.

Draw the ego state diagram as described on to flip-chart paper and explain the concept to the group.

Using an example will help them to grasp the idea and allow them to understand that as we all communicate like this, hopping between the ego states, what happens to them whilst communicating with others is perfectly natural.

The students must then complete Worksheet 2.2 in pairs and read out their answers to the rest of the group.

Put the ego states up as a display so that they can be used to analyse behaviours and events that happen in the future.

Top tips and common pitfalls

As an introduction to this topic I will ask if any students have younger siblings and when they are with them do they sometimes find that they sound like their parents. The common answer to this is 'Yes', especially if students have to look after them or get them ready to go out. This can then be explained and linked to the concepts of TA, namely it is their Parent part in operation.

Analysing our communication: an introduction to Transactional Analysis

When we communicate with others we will do so from three major parts. In TA these are called PARENT, ADULT and CHILD.

PARENT has three bits to it: Critical Parent, Controlling Parent, and Nurturing Parent. You may find yourself sounding like a PARENT with any younger brothers, sisters or cousins you have.

ADULT is the sensible part which explains things and checks these out: 'Is this the right thing to do?' As you grow up this part develops.

CHILD has two bits to it: Free Child and Rebellious Child.

As we get older all the parts stay with us – even adults can do 'free child' sometimes!

* The Critical Parent does the 'waggy finger' stuff: 'Why do you always … ?' 'Why don't you … ?'

* The Nurturing Parent does the 'well done' stuff: 'That was great!' 'Brilliant, well done you!'

* The Free Child likes the 'playing and having fun' stuff: telling jokes, messing about.

* The Rebellious Child does the 'naughty and breaking the rules' stuff: arriving late, disobeying rules.

You may catch yourself communicating using any of these parts. This is perfectly normal and will continue: Where do adults and teachers talk to you from? Are they all the same? ....
....

Look at these phrases and then work with a partner

1. **'What time is it?'**

      Answer as if in Adult i.e., sensibly...

      Answer as if in Critical Parent i.e., criticise...

      Answer as if in Free Child i.e., make a joke..

2. 'Can you lend me a ruler?'

    Answer as if in Adult...

    Answer as if in Critical Parent..

    Answer as if in Free Child...

3. 'Please will you sit down.'

    Ask this as if in Adult i.e., with a reason..

    Ask this as if in Controlling Parent i.e., tell them what to do.............................

    ....

    Ask this as if in Child...

4. 'Why have you forgotten your homework?'

    Answer as if in Adult...

    Answer as if in Critical Parent..

    Answer as if in Child..

Read out your answers and discuss them.

Can you think of other examples when you have observed these parts operating?

Photocopiable:

When explaining the ego states I use a conversation between my son and daughter as an example:

Daughter: 'That plant needs water' (in Adult)

Son: 'Yes it does, we should tell Mum' (in Adult)

Daughter reaches into the pot and rubs her hand on the soil and then moves towards my son to wipe these on to his clean school shirt (Child)

Son: 'What are you doing? Why do you always have to do something silly?' (in Parent)

Trouble ensues! As I explain this I use the diagram and ask the students which ego state is being used.

Completing the worksheet in pairs enables the students to compare what they have understood before reading out their answers.

Let them have fun with this task and allow them all to read out their answers, especially their Child responses.

Ask them for examples of interactions between themselves and adults as they will probably be able to apply their understanding quite easily.

This enables them to begin to see how voice tone and body language can influence how people perceive them.

Encourage them to be detectives over the next week and observe which ego states they can spot being used and those that they themselves use. Ask them also when and where these occur.

Teacher's notes

Worksheet 2.3: Warm fuzzies and cold pricklies (30 minutes)

Berne's work was further developed by his student Claude Steiner who examined how every interaction we have with other people leads us to receiving what he called 'strokes'. These can be either positive or negative and will not necessarily take the form of the spoken word. A list of the types of strokes available to us is on Worksheet 2.3. Being deprived of strokes can sometimes lead us to playing 'games' and 'hooking' others in order to get our stroke needs met. See Worksheet 2.4 in this session.

These worksheets allow the young people to explore the type and quality of interactions they give and receive from other people and also raise their awareness of how they 'hook' people into responding in a certain way towards them.

Display a poster of a role model or celebrity and give all the students a few Post-it notes. Ask them to write one positive comment on each of these about the individual on the poster, a warm fuzzy, and one negative comment, a cold prickly, that they think the person on the poster would receive. They must then each step forward and stick their comments on to the poster.

Following a discussion on their comments read through and complete Worksheet 2.3 and then discuss their answers as a group.

Create a warm fuzzy and cold prickly noticeboard which can be used to monitor their interactions with each other.

Warm fuzzies and cold pricklies

Strokes

Every person needs interaction with other people because we all need something called 'strokes' (this is not like stroking a cat!) and if we don't feel great it can be because of a lack of 'positive strokes'. There are four different kinds of strokes we may receive from other people.

Positive conditional strokes: for these we have had to do something. For example:

• Someone telling us we have done good work.

• Someone thanking us for helping them.

Positive unconditional strokes: for these we have not had to do anything special. For example:

• Someone smiling at us when we enter a room.

• Someone asking our opinion about something.

Negative conditional strokes: for these we have had to do something. For example:

• Being rude to someone.

• Behaving badly.

Negative unconditional strokes: for these we have not had to do anything specifically. For example:

• We may just look different.

• Someone may shout or swear at us.

The *positive strokes* are great as they lead to 'I am OK' feelings for both people involved. There is also a place for *useful negative strokes* as we learn from these and help ourselves and others to change.

Use the lists to help you answer these questions about strokes.

Strokes which make us feel uncomfortable are called

COLD PRICKLIES

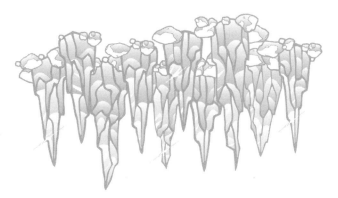

With a partner list some cold pricklies you may have received recently:

Strokes which feel good are called:

✳✳ Warm fuzzies ✳✳

☺☺☺☺☺

Now list some examples of warm fuzzies that you have received: some may be 'freebies' some you may have 'earned'.

-
-
-
-

Which of these is your favourite?

✳✳ Warm fuzzies ✳✳

Positive strokes for self and others

✳ Winking.

✳ Smiling.

✳ Asking other people their opinion or being asked ours.

✳ Making eye contact with people.

✳ Hugs.

✳ Gently patting someone on the back or arm.

✳ Using a warm voice tone when we speak.

✳ Saying thank you.

✳ Saying something nice to someone.

✳ Remembering birthdays and giving gifts.

✳ Asking how others are.

✳ Offering help and support.

✳ Having fun.

Negative strokes for self and others

- Not making eye contact.

- Staring.

- Giving someone a blank look.

- Frowning.

- Shoving, pushing, hitting someone.

- Forgetting someone's name.

- Telling jokes about people.

- Being late.

- Blaming other people.

- Interrupting someone when they are speaking.

- Sulking.

- Talking about people behind their backs.

- Shrugging when someone asks us something.

- Ignoring people.

Photocopiable:
The Behaviour Management Toolkit © Chris Parry-Mitchell, 2012 (SAGE)

Top tips and common pitfalls

Choose a poster of a recognisable celebrity for the young people to comment on.

Be prepared for viciousness and humour in their comments.

Young people will deliberately look on occasion for negative comments and it will sometimes seem uncomfortable for us to fulfil this. I have found that a negative comment delivered with a smile has the same effect and allows both parties to feel comfortable.

Case study

Lauren (12) completed this with relish, enjoying giving negative strokes to our poster celebrity. Later in the day she could be heard telling another student 'Hey, give over with the cold pricklies I need warm fuzzies as well you know!'

Teacher's notes

Worksheet 2.4: Hooks and games (30 minutes)

This develops the tasks already completed by exploring the games we play when communicating with others and how we may consciously hook people into our games so that our stroke needs can be met. The concept of people playing 'games' which are outside of conscious awareness so as to receive strokes was developed by Eric Berne (1964) in his book *Games People Play* which provides a framework for understanding the forces at work in human relationships.

Young people develop self-awareness around the topic by completing this task as they will undoubtedly do or say certain things in order to provoke a reaction from others. It allows them to realise what they are doing and acknowledge that other people act in a similar way and so helps them to normalise their actions.

Using the worksheet entitled 'Hooks and games', allow the students to note down or illustrate what they will do to get attention from people at home or in school. These include swinging on a chair, shrugging, playing stupid, etc. Once this is completed, look at each hook and examine which ego state it is attempting to engage. For example, the purpose of swinging on a chair may be to hook a nurturing parent, that is, 'Be careful you don't fall', but may actually hook a critical parent, that is, 'Will you sit on your chair properly!'

This analysis of hooks and games can be used again to self-regulate the group because attention can be drawn to it when you spot one in play. Their diagrams can be added to the wall display on Transactional Analysis.

This task can be developed further by asking the young people to notice what other people do to hook them. Hooks will come from most of the people who feature in their lives, for example the parent who complains they have had a tough day in the hope that the young person will make them a drink or help out with some of the chores.

Top tips and common pitfalls

The young people really enjoy this task and once they start their diagram it will quickly become full.

Their honesty may once again surprise you, so be careful to remain non-judgemental.

The diagram will give you an indication of the types of behaviour the young people are involved in and then you will be able to suggest more positive or appropriate ways for them to achieve the same outcome.

Complete Worksheet 2.4 with the students as it shows them how we all do this, that it is not just a teenage thing!

As they attach the ego state to each of their hooks you will probably notice a pattern. Most young people will be hooking the critical or controlling parent although occasionally, as in the swinging on the chair example, that may not have been their intention. This is a good starting point for further discussions.

The 'hook' diagrams I have seen have been very interesting and have included such things as 'bouncing my leg when Mum watches TV so she doesn't ignore me' and 'making deliberately random comments so that people will like me'. These types of statements will again give you valuable insights.

As they realise that other people will be hooking them they learn self-awareness and also that they are in control and can make their own decisions as to how they react, namely, in every situation they have the power to choose how they react to the hooks that come their way.

These tasks are some of my favourites as they can be referred back to in the future when behaviours need to be analysed and explained. They are also done with humour and respect which the students respond well to. They also enjoy pointing out to each other when Child has been used rather than Adult! Students just 'get it' and it gives them a framework for understanding how sometimes their interactions are misinterpreted and how they have the power to do things differently. I have seen young people pick this up very quickly, especially when a student said that they had spent a lesson throwing paper around the room; the initial response was laughter and then a few chorused 'Free Child' together. This response from peers is invaluable and is taken note of much quicker than hundreds of similar comments from adults!

Case study

Gary (11) filled the piece of paper with information about all the things he did to hook people. These ranged from staying silent and playing dumb to making strange noises and being the class clown. He read them all out to the group, finishing with a big sigh and saying, 'Well that's me sussed out now!'

 All photocopiable pages can be found on the CD-ROM accompanying this book.

Hooks and Games

Think about what you do at home and at school to deliberately 'HOOK' people into your 'GAMES'.

GAMES are those behaviours you do to get attention; for example I may lean back on my chair in class and HOOK the teacher because they ask me to stop or be careful … or a teacher may ask you a question and you shrug and say 'I don't know'.

Draw a HOOK diagram and list what you do: note down next to each HOOK which TA part you are HOOKING (e.g., Critical or Controlling Parent or Nurturing Parent). Which are you getting more of, warm fuzzies or cold pricklies?

3

'What makes me tick?' The differences between people

This session introduces models which are rooted in Neuro Linguistic Programming (NLP) which was developed in the USA in the 1970s by Richard Bandler and John Grinder. NLP is based on the study of human excellence; the modelling of what others do naturally and well. It allows everyone to be curious about *how* we think and behave in a variety of situations rather than *why* we do the things that we do. NLP also works from the presupposition that we can change our behaviour patterns and that if we are behaving in a way that is not useful to us, then we should do something different.

The session starts with a repeated task which allows students to recognise the successes they have had since the last session and also discusses aspects of their behaviour which have been less successful. A series of tasks follows which enables them to explore their own patterns of thinking, feeling and behaving and serves to reinforce their individuality as human beings.

Worksheet 3.1: What has gone well this week? (20 minutes)

Worksheet 3.2: Are we all taking in the same information? (20 minutes)

Worksheet 3.3: How do I tick on a bad day and a good day? (40 minutes)

Worksheet 3.4: The instant pick-me-up (15 minutes)

Timings are a guide for discussions and the completion of the relevant worksheet.

Resources required: photocopies of Worksheets 3.1, 3.2, 3.3 and 3.4; flip-chart paper; pens; pencils; rulers

Recommended further reading

O'Connor, J. (2001) *NLP Workbook – A Practical Guide to Achieving the Results You Want*, London, UK: Thorsons. This provides information on models of NLP.

Teacher's notes

Worksheet 3.1: What has gone well this week? (20 minutes)

This worksheet helps to develop an individual's self-esteem and is done on a weekly basis. It enables the students to reflect on what has happened during the past week.

Individuals who have good self-esteem can notice all the small steps that they make along the way in achieving a goal. However those who have lower self-esteem rather than noting their own progress will tend to constantly compare themselves to a perceived expert and will therefore never feel they have achieved. This task thus begins to reinforce for the students the positive aspects of their behaviour and allows for praise to be received from the group.

The worksheet is completed by the students individually and once this has been done the written contributions for each section are discussed as a group, starting with the positive aspects. This allows for praise to be received and some discussion and analysis to occur in a safe environment of the less positive aspects of their week. Completing this task each session with a group has the effect of ensuring the students are noticing aspects of their life, namely, the small steps, which are going well or are positive and this then helps them develop their self-esteem.

Once discussed, the students must select one example from the top of their worksheet and illustrate this. It is then used for a wallchart with their name attached, which will illustrate their progress over the rest of the sessions.

Top tips and common pitfalls

Students are not always good at writing down what has gone well and may need some prompting. I usually give them a few examples verbally of the things they could include and this seems to encourage them to think of other things. For example, 'arrived at school on time, stayed in lessons, remembered equipment or sports kit'.

Some students for whatever reason will have difficult weeks and when this happens ask them to think of anything that has gone well, from speaking politely to just one person (even if it is you), to making a parent a cup of coffee or keeping their room tidy.

Pay close attention to the students when they are filling in the worksheet so that you can prompt and assist those who may be struggling.

When the students read out their examples to the group remind them of the ground rules and enforce these as necessary.

Praise, clap, cheer as appropriate for all the positive things they note down!

Ask the group for verbal feedback as appropriate on the less positive aspects of the week. Keep the discussion on this part of the worksheet moving so it doesn't become competitive, namely, on whose behaviour has been the worst. The students will attempt to justify their behaviour so keep your feedback to them non-judgemental and evidence-based if possible.

What has gone well this week?

Name:

Thinking about this last week at school and at home list three things that have '**gone well**'. ☺☺☺

Possible ideas: you had a good lesson/day; you completed some work in class; you completed some homework; you spoke politely to people; you have been on time ...

1.

2.

3.

Choose your best one from these three and draw it on a piece of paper.

Now write down any things that 'haven't gone as well' this week. ☺☹☺

1.

2.

3.

Photocopiable:
The Behaviour Management Toolkit © Chris Parry-Mitchell, 2012 (SAGE)

Teacher's notes

Worksheet 3.2: Are we all taking in the same information? (30 minutes)

This is a discussion and written task to enable the young people to begin to under-stand that as human beings we are different on the inside from what we look like on the outside. This allows them to understand their preferences for taking in informa-tion about their surroundings and from other people and how these preferences will influence the choices they make. It may also explain to them why they will fall out with some people and thus enable them to avoid conflict by understanding these differences. Within education the terms auditory, visual and kinaesthetic have been used to describe types of learner. This session's tasks take this a step further by allow-ing them to understand that it is not just a learning style but also our individual and unique way of filtering and making sense of all the information we receive from the world every second.

This is done by first drawing a face containing only the eyebrows on the flip chart. The young people are then asked questions which will allow them to identify the senses which enable us as human beings to take in information about our surround-ings, namely, seeing, hearing, smelling, tasting and touching. Eyes, ears, a nose, a mouth and a hand are then added to the flip-chart picture.

The students must then complete Worksheet 3.2. Part One needs to be completed silently and individually. Once finished they can move on to Part Two which allows them to compare answers with a partner and see how many items on their lists are *exactly the same*. Part Three then asks them to score their preferences and develop an understanding of what this actually means.

Top tips and common pitfalls

When I ask student to complete these tasks I use the analogy of us having invisible masks on our faces, rather like those used in fencing. The idea is that some pieces of information I receive from the outside world will go straight through whilst other pieces will hit the mesh and bounce off depending on how my individual mask is set. As we have millions of pieces of sensory information coming at us every second and we can only pay conscious attention to between five and nine, we have to have a filter or mask system otherwise we would be overloaded!

When they have worked out their preference I write all the individual scores for visual (V), auditory (A) and kinaesthetic (K) on a list. This can make for very interesting read-ing and help explain a few behaviours.

The most important thing to convey to the students is that all of the filters are equal.

Ask them to think of people they know and guess which preference they have. Which preference does the person at home who always wants things tidy have? Which prefer-ence does the adult who notices when voices are raised or music is on too loud have? Which preference does the person who cannot concentrate if they are too hot or too cold have? They then become able to spot these preferences and use that information.

Are we all taking in the same information?

We are going to do an experiment to find out if we are all taking in the same information. As we are here together we are taking in all sorts of information through our senses: sight, hearing, smell, taste and touch. For PART ONE of this experiment you are going to list the first 12 things that you notice through your senses as you sit here now.

1.

2.

3.

4.

5.

6.

7.

8.

9.

10.

11.

12.

PART TWO: When you have completed your list find a partner and put a tick next to each answer you have that is exactly the same as your partner's. How many do you have that are the same? Make sure these are *exactly* the same.

Note that it is usual for people to have none the same!

PART THREE: Now go through your own list and mark next to each of your answers whether it was something you could see, something you could hear, something you could smell, or something you could taste or touch. If it was something seen put 'V for VISUAL' next to it; if it was something heard put 'A for AUDITORY' next to it; and if it was smelt, tasted or felt put 'K for KINAESTHETIC' next to it.

How many Vs, As and Ks do you have?

V:

A:

K:

So we now know that we all take in different pieces of information depending on whether our filters are set for visual, auditory or kinaesthetic. Look at the table below and see if the results of the experiment are correct about you. Are you clearly one of these or a mixture?

Mostly visual	**Mostly auditory**	**Mostly kinaesthetic**
I like colourful, sparkly clothes.	Loud noises irritate me.	I like comfortable clothes. Labels annoy me.
I like things to be neat and tidy most of the time.	I can remember exactly what people have said to me, word for word.	I like to doodle and get up and move about.
I notice what other people are wearing.	I don't always look at people when they talk to me.	I don't like to be too hot or too cold.
I can talk quite fast.	I like listening to music.	I get a 'gut' feeling whether I like someone or not.

How your filters are set influences how you take in information from the world. No one filter is better than the other, just different. Our filters can influence:

- our likes and dislikes;

- our language: e.g., Visual 'Do you **see** what I mean?';

- what we value;

- what presents we like. What would you buy someone with a strong visual, auditory, or kinaesthetic filter?

Think about some of the people in your life. How do you think their filters are set?

Photocopiable:
The Behaviour Management Toolkit © Chris Parry-Mitchell, 2012 (SAGE)

Most of the young people who have attended the programme have had a kinaesthetic preference: they are the doodlers, the wanderers in the classroom, the ones that get into trouble for prodding or hitting others.

Case studies

Beth (15) completed these tasks and discovered she had a very strong kinaesthetic preference. Whilst discussing the task she suddenly got up and produced a pair of slipper socks from her bag. She then announced that of course as she was kinaesthetic it would now be acceptable for her take her shoes off and put her slipper socks on! She did so with a huge sigh of relief and brought them with her to every subsequent session.

Dan (14) was always getting in to trouble for chattering. When he completed the task he came out with a very strong auditory preference. 'This explains the chattering' he said, as 'I can only hear my voice and no one else's!'

Teacher's notes

Section 3: Worksheet 3.3: 'How do I tick on a bad day and a good day?' (40 minutes)

This task enables the young people to analyse how they think, feel and behave on two different types of day. It is based on the NLP model which Bandler and Grinder used to map human excellence as they worked with family therapist Virginia Satir, founder of Gestalt Theory, Fritz Pearls, and the hypnotherapist Milton Erickson.

Completion of these worksheets allows the young people to develop their self-awareness whilst also understanding the connection between their minds and bodies. It means that they will begin to realise that they have control over what they think and feel and can therefore choose how to respond or behave, thereby enabling them to be more in control of situations.

First draw a circle dissected into three equal parts on to the flip-chart paper. One section should be labelled 'Internal thinking', namely, self-talk, the next 'Internal feeling', and the third 'External behaviour', namely, the behaviours someone else would see. After explaining how these sections all inter-relate using an example, the students must complete the two worksheets starting with 'A bad day'. Discussions about what they have written need to take place after each section.

Once completed, the worksheets can be displayed individually or a group one can be created for 'A good day'.

'How do I tick on a bad day and a good day?'

Task: Divide the circle into three equal sections. Use the three sections to model how you have a '**bad day**'.

Section 1: **Internal thinking**: What would you be thinking? What would you be saying to yourself on the inside? What would you be picturing? Are there any sounds?

Section 2: **Internal feeling**: How would you be feeling?

Section 3: **External behaviour**: How would you be behaving? How would someone know you were having a bad day? What would they actually see? (Facial expression, eye movements, gestures, posture, breathing?)

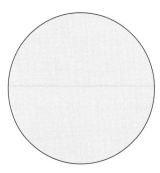

Task: Divide the circle into three equal sections. Now use the three sections to work out how you have a '**good day**'.

Section 1: **Internal thinking**: What would you be thinking? What would you be saying to yourself on the inside? What would you be picturing? Are there any sounds?

Section 2: **Internal feeling**: How would you be feeling?

Section 3: **External behaviour**: How would you be behaving? How would someone know you were having a good day? What would they actually see? (Facial expression, eye movements, gestures, posture, breathing?)

Top tips and common pitfalls

Use the example of going to work to explain the model which has been drawn on the flip chart: namely, internal thinking 'Oh no, work! I have so much to do!' or internal feelings of dread and sadness with their characteristic behaviour: a sigh, a sad face, head down, etc. Students usually love this as you can make it as personal to the group as necessary. Start with a bad day and then do the same for a good day.

When they complete the worksheets the bad day should be finished first as they will find this one easier to complete and can then imagine a good day by writing down opposites if necessary.

Ask them to think of a typical good day which need not be related to their choice of bad day.

Keep the pace of the work moving forward. If too much time is spent on the bad day, students will begin to compare whose bad day was the worst and the mood of the group will be affected.

Teacher's notes

Worksheet 3.4: The instant pick-me-up (15 minutes)

This is a practical task which allows the young people to experience practically how their external behaviour (posture, breathing, direction of eyes and facial expression) impacts on their thoughts and feelings.

Completing this allows them to further develop their understanding of the connection between mind and body and this is a useful thing to know. They are also reminded that only they can choose how they stand or sit and by simply altering their external behaviour things will begin to feel different.

Once they have undergone the physical experiences listed on the worksheet they can then discuss where these might be of use.

Top tips and common pitfalls

I usually complete Parts One and Two as a group activity and students are often very capable of sitting as if they were bored and fed up! As they do this, I provide a commentary of what they may be saying to themselves, namely, their internal thinking, and they will then associate more with the experience.

This task can be done in pairs so they can then help each other to develop a walking style that exhibits confidence and poise.

Have a 'walk off' where they can show their confident walk to the staff. This will be rather interesting!

Set them a home play task to walk to the worst lesson of the week with their head held high and a smile on their face and notice how this feels.

The instant pick-me-up

We know that our thoughts and feelings and our external behaviour are all linked and that these affect each other ... so when we change one it then has a knock on effect and they will all change! You can use this trick when you are feeling fed up or in need of a confidence boost.

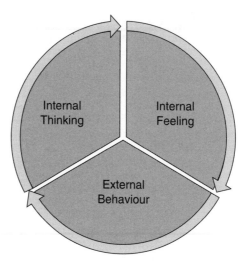

The easiest one to change is our external behaviour. By this we mean: posture, gestures, facial expression, direction of eyes and breathing.

1. Have a go at sitting as if you were really bored and fed up; now try to sit as if you were really interested and feeling good. Can you feel the difference?

2. Stand as if you are really fed up and feeling miserable. How does this feel?

3. Stand up really tall and straight. Focus your eyes ahead of you. Put your shoulders back and breathe normally; now walk like this. How do you feel? When and where might this positive way of walking be useful to you?

Case study

Simon (13) completed this task and then went off to experiment for the week. On his return he announced that it had got him into trouble. How? He explained that when he had strutted into his classroom with a big smiling face and put his hand up to High Five a teacher had immediately responded with 'Out!' When he demonstrated this to us I can see how it happened. Remind the students it is neither a walk, nor a strut, nor a swagger, nor the sort of walk which gives the impression of carrying a carpet under each arm!

 All photocopiable pages can be found on the CD-ROM accompanying this book.

4

Hitting the targets: setting goals and examining meanings

This session introduces the work of Albert Mehrabian which was developed in the 1960s. He identified that when we communicate with others we take emotional meaning from three areas: words, the way the words are said, and non-verbal communication. This is important for young people to understand and especially during the teenage years when shrugging and grunting can replace more usual forms of communication. Following this, an overview of the change process is introduced alongside a goal-setting strategy with a difference. These allow young people to see how a change in behaviour comes about whilst also setting an achievable and motivating goal that is related to their own behaviours, creating the evidence they will see, hear and feel on its successful completion.

The session starts with a repeated task which allows students to recognise the successes they have had since the last session and also discusses aspects of their behaviour which have been less successful. A series of tasks related to the work of Mehrabian, a process for change and goal setting are then completed.

Worksheet 4.1:   What has gone well this week? (20 minutes)

Worksheet 4.2:   What am I meaning? (20 minutes)

Worksheet 4.3:   What did they 'actually' mean? (20 minutes)

Worksheet 4.4:   Setting and hitting the target (40 minutes)

Timings are a guide for discussions and the completion of the relevant worksheet.

Resources required: photocopies of Worksheets 4.1, 4.2, 4.3 and 4.4; flip-chart paper; pens; pencils; felt pens; rulers

Recommended further reading

Mehrabian, A. (1972) *Nonverbal Communication,* The Hague: Walter De Guyter. This provides more information about Albert Mehrabian's research.

Teacher's notes

Worksheet 4.1: What has gone well this week? (20 minutes)

This worksheet helps to develop an individual's self-esteem and is done on a weekly basis. It enables the students to reflect on what has happened during the past week.

Individuals who have good self-esteem can notice all the small steps that they make along the way to achieving their goal. However those who have lower self-esteem rather than noting their own progress, tend to constantly compare themselves to a perceived expert and therefore will never feel they have achieved. This task thus begins to reinforce for the students the positive aspects of their behaviour and allows for praise to be received from the group.

The worksheet is completed by the students individually and once this has been done the written contributions for each section are discussed as a group, starting with the positive aspects. This allows for praise to be received and some discussion and analysis to occur in a safe environment of the less positive aspects of their week. Completing this task each session with a group has the effect of ensuring the students are noticing those aspects of their life, namely, the small steps, that are going well or are positive and this helps them to develop their self-esteem.

Once discussed, the students must select one example from the top of their worksheet and illustrate this. It is then used on a wallchart with their name attached, which follows their progress over the rest of the sessions.

Top tips and common pitfalls

Students are not always good at writing down what has gone well and may need some prompting. I usually give them a few examples verbally of the things they could write down and these seem to encourage them to think of other things. For example, 'arrived at school on time, stayed in lessons, remembered equipment or sports kit'.

Some students for whatever reason will have difficult weeks and when this happens ask them to think of anything that has gone well, from speaking politely to just one person (even if it is you), to making a parent a cup of coffee or keeping their room tidy.

Pay close attention to the students when they are filling in the worksheet so that you can prompt and assist those who may be struggling.

When the students read out their examples to the group remind them of the ground rules and enforce these as necessary.

Praise, clap, cheer as appropriate for all the positive things they have noted down!

Ask the group for verbal feedback as appropriate on the less positive aspects of the week. Keep the discussions on this part of the worksheet moving so they don't become competitive, namely, whose behaviour has been the worst. The students will attempt to justify their behaviour so keep your feedback to them non-judgemental and evidence-based if possible.

What has gone well this week?

Name:

Thinking about this last week at school and at home list three things that have '**gone well**'. ☺☺☺

Possible ideas: you had a good lesson/day; you completed some work in class; you completed some homework; you spoke politely to people; you have been on time …

1.

2.

3.

Choose your best one from these three and draw it on a piece of paper.

Now write down any things that 'haven't gone as well' this week. ☺☹☺

1.

2.

3.

Teacher's notes

Worksheet 4.2: What am I meaning? (20 minutes)

Albert Mehrabian's research in the 1960s examined where people take meaning from in communications expressing feelings and attitudes. His interpretation was that 7 per cent is taken from the words that are spoken, 38 per cent from the way the words are said, and 55 per cent from non-verbal communication. We pay conscious attention to the words which are spoken unless, of course, the voice tone and non-verbal communication are unusual! Young people are often judged by their non-verbal communication and voice tone, that is, we can all describe the stereotypical grunting and shrugging teen. This discussion and practical task enables them to experience the research by Mehrabian for themselves in a safe and structured way and to begin to understand the impact of any grunting or shrugging!

List the three factors on flip-chart paper and discuss with the students what we mean by each of them, especially non-verbal communication/body language. Ask them to list these in order of importance when communicating or interacting with others.

Using the worksheet as a guide say the word 'really' in turn, first just altering the voice tone and then by adding some facial expression and other non-verbal communication. A discussion can then follow as to how the meaning of the word changes depending on how it is said. Other words such as 'yes', 'no' and 'sorry' can then be experimented on.

Have a discussion on how we can best use our voice tone and non-verbal communication to ensure we get on better with other people or as preparation when we have to have a difficult conversation with someone.

Top tips and common pitfalls

I usually introduce this task by asking students if they have ever had a text or email and got annoyed with the person sending it because of the tone of voice it was written in! The work by Mehrabian goes some way to explain this, as with the written word alone we only have 7 per cent of the meaning and we therefore tend to put our own interpretation of voice tone and non-verbal communication to this, and then feel aggrieved!

This is a fun task although the young people may find it difficult initially as they can feel inhibited. Usually, as staff join in, being as dramatic as possible, students will relax and have fun with it.

Complete the 'really' task first whilst they are sitting on their hands. This ensures they understand how difficult it is to keep a straight face.

This concept can be reinforced throughout the session by noticing young people's voice tones and non-verbal communication and feeding this back to them with a smile.

What am I meaning?

Have you ever reacted to someone's email or text message? Perhaps by thinking 'Who do they think they are talking to?'

This can be explained by the work of communication researcher, Professor Albert Mehrabian. He discovered that people take meaning from three areas that can be divided up like this:

- Non-verbal communication or body language e.g., facial expression, gesture, eye movement, posture: 55%

- Voice tone and quality: 38%

- Words: 7%

Are you surprised by this?

This therefore explains the misunderstanding with the text or email, doesn't it? We have only the words so we only have 7% of the meaning: we therefore add our own voice tone and quality and non-verbal communications ... usually the wrong ones.

- Think about how many different ways you can say the word 'really'. Change the volume, pitch, speed and emphasis of your voice as you say the word and add some body language. Does this make a difference to the meaning of the word? What about the words 'yes,' 'no' and 'sorry'?

- How much notice do you take of other people's body language? What do you assume from different people's faces when they look at you? How might this play out at home or school?

Teacher's notes

Worksheet 4.3: What did they 'actually' mean? (20 minutes)

This task is aimed at enabling young people to think about a difficult situation they have experienced but from another person's involved perspective. Most will operate from the 'self-' position and rarely think things through using another's viewpoint. It is a useful skill, therefore, to develop and it also reinforces the fact that in reality we can only assume and guess why other people behave the way they do. It links in with one of the NLP's presuppositions which states that 'behaviour has a positive intention'. This can be difficult to grasp and live with as it assumes that a person's behaviour makes sense to them on some level – even the most challenging behaviour you may observe.

Completing the worksheet with a discussion after each section allows the group to feedback on each other's situations and enables them to develop further the idea that there are wide and differing reasons for why people behave as they do.

Following on from the worksheet, broaden the discussion to look at any other issues they may be involved in or aware of.

Top tips and common pitfalls

Be ready for their honesty about a situation in A and C.

As they read out their scenarios in A, pay attention to what it is said as sometimes what starts out as bravado can quickly lead to bad feeling.

Keep the discussion moving and the young people on task as they will always be ready to join in and reinforce for each other how bad a situation was, especially in the parts marked A and B.

When completing B I usually ask them to think of a positive and a negative reason why the other person behaved as they did. The negative reason can be over the top, for example 'Well they obviously hate you!' This usually brings the response 'No they don't' and from there the discussion can become more constructive as they analyse why the other person behaved as they did. Use this tactic wisely and only with good rapport.

Avoid making judgements.

Case study

Matthew (16) completed this task by stating that he had fallen out with his sister (fine as a scenario so far) and then pushed her into the wardrobe and locked it, leaving her there for an hour (now not an appropriate scenario). Not being judgemental in this instance was very difficult. The group gave him some honest teenage feedback and he became initially defensive and then upset. In Section C, he decided on how he should have handled the situation differently and also decided that he needed to apologise to his sister which he then did. (All's well that ends well.)

What did they 'actually' mean?

Think of a situation when you didn't agree with someone.

A: List the facts.

-

-

-

B: Think of three possible meanings for why the other person behaved as they did.

1.

2.

3.

C: Think about your behaviour. Did you play a part in what happened? How could you have done things differently?

-

-

-

-

Remember that we can never truly know why somebody behaved as they did. We can only guess. If we believe that all behaviour makes sense to the person involved, does this help us look at situations differently?

Teacher's notes

Worksheet 4.4: Setting and hitting the target (40 minutes)

This task involves setting a goal whilst also gathering enough evidence to make it compelling and motivating. As has been suggested (Locke, 1968) goal setting and motivation are linked and this process enables young people to set themselves a realistic goal around a behaviour and create some compelling evidence of what it will actually be like for them once they have achieved it.

The fact that they must metaphorically transport themselves to the future when they have achieved their goal makes them more determined to succeed. Encouraging them to use this process regularly enables them to be more able to set and achieve goals around lots of different things.

Write the overview of the task on to the flip-chart paper and take them through the process step by step using an example of your own. The goal must be stated as a positive (e.g., 'I want to arrive at school on time' rather than 'I don't want to be late'). This is because in the second statement we have to process and visualise being late and then process the don't, that is, we cannot not think of something. Go through the worksheet slowly discussing relevant points as necessary. The visual, auditory and kinaesthetic evidence is vital here and needs to be as clear and compelling as possible as it is this that motivates us to succeed.

When the task is complete, give each student a piece of paper on which they can write their name and goal plus the visual, auditory, and kinaesthetic evidence they will have accumulated in achieving this. They can then decorate all of these for display.

Top tips and common pitfalls

Make sure the goals are realistic.

The evidence needs to be compelling, namely, enough for them to want it now. With the visual evidence encourage them to note what others will be like when they have achieved it, that is, smiling and making positive comments.

The final point of consequences for the self and others or 'ecology' may need to be discussed as young people can be unwilling to change their behaviour if their friends or peers rely on them behaving in a certain way. For example, if I suddenly stop being the class clown how will my friends feel about me? This can be balanced to a certain extent by asking how significant adults will feel if they improve their behaviour, but remember that the peer group is more important to young people.

Encourage them to share their goal with others so that they provide themselves with a support network should it become difficult to maintain; remind them that if they do begin to fail then they should dust themselves down and start again.

Setting and hitting the target

This process will help us to be clear about what we want and also specific about what we will see, hear and feel when we have achieved our goal.

P Positive: State what you want. Remember that this must be written as a positive: 'I want ...'. This is because our brain doesn't hear don't instructions. (What happens if you *don't* think about a piece of chocolate cake?)

I want ...

O Own part: What will you do exactly? Remember this is about you.

I will ...

S Specific: When? Where? How? Who with? Be specific.

S Size: Is this goal the right size? If it is too large, break it down into smaller goals that are clear and achievable and start again.

E Evidence: How will you know when you have achieved your goal? What will you see, hear and feel?

I will see ...

I will hear ...

I will feel ...

E Ecology: Are there any consequences from having this goal for you or other people? Sometimes other people are affected when we change. Will achieving this goal affect other parts of your life? If you could have it right now, would you take it?

Case studies

Rebecca (14) completed this task about stopping smoking and when it came to the ecology check she did stop, because for her, smoking was a way to relieve the stress of having an alcoholic parent. Further work had to be done to provide her with a better way to relieve that stress which was less harmful to her than smoking.

Luke (12) completed this task about getting to school on time. He shared it with the school office staff so that he had a few people to remind him of what he had set out to achieve and they were on hand to prompt him if he started to wander in late again.

 All photocopiable pages can be found on the CD-ROM accompanying this book.

5

Keeping it real: understanding anger and strategies to help

This session examines 'anger' and aims to enable young people to understand that it is perfectly normal to feel angry as anger is one of a range of human emotions. The concept that anger may have evolutionary, physiological and emotional components is explained and discussed. This series of tasks is based on the work of neurologists and psychotherapists Paul Maclean (1990), David Grove and B.I. Panzer (1989) and Caitlin Walker (1997).

Young people can often feel controlled by their anger or tempers and this can then colour their responses to situations as well as their ability to interact with others. Gaining an understanding of the components of their tempers helps them realise that they are just the same as others and that they actually have control of their responses rather than regarding 'it' as uncontrollable.

The session starts with a repeated task which allows students to recognise the successes they have had since the last session and also discusses aspects of their behaviour which have been less successful. The worksheets which follow initially analyse the students' anger patterns and then outline two practical strategies they can use to take control.

Worksheet 5.1:   What has gone well this week? (20 minutes)

Worksheet 5.2:   Our brains and anger (20 minutes)

Worksheet 5.3:   The anger path (10 minutes)

Worksheet 5.4:   What is my anger like? (40 minutes)

Worksheet 5.5:   Bin it ... I am in control (30 minutes)

Worksheet 5.6:   Breathing round the square (5 minutes)

Timings are a guide for discussions and the completion of the relevant worksheet.

Resources required: photocopies of Worksheets 5.1, 5.2, 5.3, 5.4, 5.5 and 5.6; flip-chart paper; paper; pens; pencils; felt pens; rulers

Recommended further reading

Walker, C. (1987) *Clean Language and Systemic Modelling,* Training Attention DVD. www. amberfilms.co.uk. A useful resource available from www.trainingattention.com which provides simple exercises using Clean Language.

Teacher's notes

Worksheet 5.1: What has gone well this week? (20 minutes)

This worksheet helps to develop an individual's self-esteem and is done on a weekly basis. It enables the students to reflect on what has happened during the past week.

Individuals who have good self-esteem can notice all the small steps that they make along the way in achieving a goal. However those who have lower self-esteem rather than noting their own progress can tend to constantly compare themselves to a perceived expert and therefore will never feel they have achieved. This task thus begins to reinforce for the students the positive aspects of their behaviour and allows for praise to be received from the group.

The worksheet is completed by the students individually and once this has been done the written contributions to each section will be discussed as a group, starting with the positive aspects. This allows for praise to be received and some discussion and analysis to occur regarding the less positive aspects of their week, in a safe environment. Completing this task each session with a group has the effect of ensuring the students are noticing those aspects of their life, namely, the small steps, that are going well or are positive and so this helps them develop their self-esteem.

Once discussed, the students must select one example from the top of their worksheet and illustrate this. It is then used for a wallchart with their name attached which will follow their progress over the remaining sessions.

Top tips and common pitfalls

Students are not always good at writing down what has gone well and may need some prompting. I usually give them a few examples verbally of the things they could write down and these seem to encourage them to think of other things. For example, 'arrived at school on time, stayed in lessons, remembered equipment or sports kit'.

Some students for whatever reason will have difficult weeks and when this happens ask them to think of anything that has gone well, from speaking politely to just one person (even if it is you), to making a parent a cup of coffee or keeping their room tidy.

Pay close attention to the students when they are filling in the worksheet so that you can prompt and assist those who may be struggling.

When the students read out their examples to the group remind them of the ground rules and enforce these as necessary.

Praise, clap, cheer as appropriate for all the positive things they note down!

What has gone well this week?

Name:

Thinking about this last week at school and at home list three things that have '**gone well**'. ☺☺☺

Possible ideas: you had a good lesson/day; you completed some work in class; you completed some homework; you spoke politely to people; you have been on time ...

1.

2.

3.

Choose your best one from these three and draw it on a piece of paper.

Now write down any things that 'haven't gone as well' this week. ☺☹☺

1.

2.

3.

Photocopiable:

The Behaviour Management Toolkit © Chris Parry-Mitchell, 2012 (SAGE)

Ask the group for verbal feedback as appropriate on the less positive aspects of the week. Keep the discussions on this part of the worksheet moving so they don't become competitive, namely, about whose behaviour has been the worst. The students will attempt to justify their behaviour so keep your feedback to them non-judgemental and evidence-based if possible.

Teacher's notes

Worksheet 5.2: Our brains and anger (20 minutes)

In the 1970s, neurologist Paul Maclean proposed a model called the 'triune brain' whereby the brain can be divided into three parts with the oldest being the 'reptilian' brain. This brain is related to our fight or flight response and is triggered whenever we feel threatened or are tired, as well as frightened, hungry and cold. Whenever we have to manage young people's behaviour, we are dealing with their reptilian brain.

The other two parts are the 'mammalian brain' and the 'neo cortex'. The mammalian brain can be triggered if people behave in a way that we feel is unacceptable, as constrained by our views of society, like someone trying to get into a lift before the lift has emptied. People should just know that shouldn't be done! The neo cortex is the part we access whenever we are learning something new. However, we can only access this brain if the other two parts are content, that is, we need to feel safe (reptilian brain) and we need to know the rules and boundaries (mammalian brain) and then we can learn.

Using the flip-chart paper first draw a small circle and label this 'reptilian brain'. Then draw another slightly bigger circle on top of it starting from the same base point and label this 'mammalian brain'. Finally draw a slightly bigger circle again starting from the same base point and label this 'neo cortex'. Discuss with students the relevance of each part of the brain.

The worksheet can then be completed, thus enabling them to begin to examine their reptilian brains, that is, what makes them very, very angry!

Top tips and common pitfalls

When introducing this topic I normally tell students a story about how evolution theory suggests we are the descendants of cavemen and therefore when a raptor dinosaur was wandering past my cave entrance one morning I found myself with three choices. First, I could choose to beat it over the head with my club and have dinosaur steak for tea and make a nice dinosaur handbag; this would be my fight response. Second, I could opt for screaming, running and then hiding at the back of my cave until it had passed; this would be my flight response. Third, I could just stand open-mouthed at the entrance of the cave and be paralysed by fear; my freeze response. This story helps students understand the fight or flight response and they seem to enjoy the idea of dinosaurs and cavemen.

Our brains and anger

Anger is perfectly natural. The part of our brain which is responsible for anger is linked to a time when we were cavemen; it is sometimes called our reptilian brain and is our fight or flight response that has been designed to keep us safe. This part of our brain gets involved when we feel threatened or when we are hungry, cold, tired, frightened, etc. This can be one large outburst of anger or it can simmer for a while before we lose it!

What sorts of things send you into this *caveman* brain?

When discussing anger, I start with the put your hand up scenarios, namely, 'Who here gets angry?' Hands go up. 'Who shouts and swears?' Hands go up. 'Who is a door slammer?' 'Who has to have the last word?' 'Who cries when they are really angry?' 'Who hits things?', etc. This enables the young people to see that it is a natural human emotion, especially when adults join in, and then they will become more open about discussing the worksheet.

Be aware that young people can sometimes be frightened by their tempers so avoid making sweeping judgemental statements about 'angry' people.

Have a good-humoured discussion about what makes them angry and you will find common ground which can be useful for creating rapport.

In the future, when they tell stories of how angry they became in a situation, refer to this as 'Captain Caveman being at it again.' This results in them beginning to understand that being angry is just a part of them and not all of who they are.

Case study

After hearing the introduction on the triune brain, Jake (12) just nodded at me. He had understood why in his previous Food Tech lesson he had kicked the table, sworn at the teacher, and run off. The lesson had started with him not having the ingredients for the set recipe. He was told off by the teacher and asked to sit down and get his pen out as he would be copying out the recipe again. Jake had no pen so this prompted another reprimand. The teacher gave him a pen, some paper and the recipe book at which point Jake, after sitting and looking at it for a minute, completely lost it. He threw down the book, paper and pen, kicked the desk away, swore, and stomped off. This, he had now realised, was a reptilian brain response. Why? Jake had very poor literacy skills and therefore being asked to read and write, something he felt very threatened by, resulted in first fight and then flight!

Teacher's notes

Worksheet 5.3: The anger path (10 minutes)

This is a discussion task which explains to the young person what happens physiologically when we get angry. This continues to develop their understanding that it is a normal human emotion and whilst it may sometimes feel that it is out of our control there are points along the path to 'losing it' when we are still in control – and can therefore use strategies to keep us safe.

Draw the anger path on the flip chart, discussing each step and asking the young people for their own personal experiences as well as answering any questions they may have.

When finished move on to Worksheet 5.4.

The anger path

When we get angry our body reacts like this ...

1. We are OK. ☺

2. Something triggers us to feel a bit niggled: our heart rate starts to increase and the hormone adrenaline starts to be released. We are still in control.

3. Something else triggers us. We are still in control.

4. We reach our anger point of no return.

5. We get angry in our own way. Our fight or flight response has kicked in and we lose it!

6. We calm down and have to face any consequences.

7. We are OK. ☺

Does it sometimes feel that you go straight from 2 to 5?

Physiologically that is possible, as the adrenaline release will be instantaneous because you feel threatened; however, now you can understand what happens you can take more control of your tempers.

Points 6 to 7 can take at least 20 minutes because the adrenaline has to be diluted.

Top tips and common pitfalls

Avoid being shocked by what students say.

Keep the discussions moving so that these do not become a competition for who has the worst and most violent temper.

Join in and let them know how your temper pans out.

Some may tell you that they will go straight to number five. When this happens, explain slowly all the things that have to take place in the body up to the point when adrenaline is released. I have found by telling them this at a slow rate it somehow convinces them that this can't happen instantaneously, so they are then in control longer and have more time to adopt another strategy.

Discuss with them the fact that as they get older, the consequences for getting angry and aggressive become more serious. This may start with a push and a punch from another person when they first start school which then leads to missing break sometimes. However, a push and a punch on the street at age 21 would probably lead to their being arrested.

Teacher's notes

Worksheet 5.4: What is my anger like? (40 minutes)

This is a modelling task based initially on the work of David Grove, James Lawley and Penny Tompkinson, who in 1996 ran their first 'Clean Language' joint trainings that were later developed by Caitlin Walker. The use of questions based on Clean Language avoids the contamination of ideas and encourages young people to develop their own unique understanding of a concept; in this case their anger. There is a belief that as human beings we always know more than we think we know.

Completing this worksheet enables students to understand that their anger is just a part of them and not who they are. It also helps them to turn the concept of their temper into a metaphor and analyse what happens to them every step of the way as well as what they need from others as they get angry and then calm down. Progressing through the task allows them to draw out what their temper actually looks like and where it is located. All of this can then be displayed.

Top tips and common pitfalls

Complete this worksheet with the young people. They can then understand how this works for another person and discover any commonalities.

If they struggle with bullet point 4 on the worksheet, that is, 'It is like ...' I will usually ask them if it is like a fluffy bunny skipping along on a warm sunny day. They will immediately say 'No', so I will then follow with, 'OK, so what is it like then?' and usually they will explain this or start drawing. Once their drawing is complete, ask them to write down what it is and where it is located.

What is my anger like?

Our temper is just a part of us so let's find out about it by filling in the spaces:

- Think of the word you use to describe yourself when you get angry. What is it? Write it here '............'

- I get '............' the most when I am at/in...................................

- I never get '............' when I am at/in/with...................................

Describe it ...

- When I am starting to get '............' it is like...

- This part of me looks like this. (Draw it on a separate piece of paper, describe it and say where this part is.)

- The first thing that lets me know I am getting '............' is ...

- What happens next is ...

- When I am at my worst I am like ...

- The first thing someone else would notice about me is ...

- Someone could make it worse by ...

- Someone could help me by ...

Calming down ...

- I need this to calm down ...

Explain that there are no incorrect answers as our anger and temper are unique to us. Be prepared for a range of images, some of which will be very insightful.

Asking students to think of a recent scenario when they felt angry helps them to understand the order of what happens to them.

Spend an equal amount of time on each section. Do not neglect the calming-down section.

Allow them time to write down their answers for each section and then ask them to read these back to each other if appropriate. Be prepared for detailed discussions of what happens to each of them. Remember to let them speak.

Case studies

The first time I completed this with a group George (13) sat next me. We got to the question asking us to draw it out and he turned to me and said, 'It's big, it's round and it's in here', and he pointed to his stomach. The look on his face conveyed surprise at being asked such an obvious question and how stupid I was that I didn't know that!

Amy (15) spent a long time drawing her temper and when she revealed it the paper was covered in a large, blue, wiggly worm. Asked to explain this, she said this thing started at the base of her spine and wiggled its way from side to side up her back to her neck where it started to shake.

Teacher's notes

Worksheet 5.5: Bin it ... I am in control (30 minutes)

This worksheet is based on the concept of submodalities or the fine and subtle details of our inner representations and how we can change them in order to feel better about a situation. It is a strategy we can use for reducing or minimising negative feelings after an argument or one we can adopt as the young person begins to recognise that they are getting angry. The task allows them to experience a strategy they could practise and use when they are still in control and before they have headed down on the Anger Path.

It comes from the work of John Grinder in 1983, one of the founders of NLP, who used the idea of changing the qualities of our inner thoughts and feelings to create the motivation to change beliefs and behaviours. Grinder, along with Richard Bandler, created a representational system of our experiences explaining how as human beings we describe our experiences to ourselves and others using our different senses: namely, a memory of a day trip may be in colour or black and white and it may have sounds attached to it which may be loud or soft.

The worksheet is completed in pairs with one student asking the questions and then recording the responses of their partner. The students need to sit side by side as they do this task as the individual who is answering the questions will be thinking to themselves how the situation is represented. If the partner asking the questions is sitting directly in front of them, this may put them off.

Once the task is completed, the students must change roles. Only when both have completed the task should they discuss their answers with each other so as to avoid a transfer of ideas and thoughts.

Once completed, a discussion as to when and where this strategy could be used should follow. Referring back to the Anger Path will enable the young person to understand when this should be used so as to avoid losing it.

Top tips and common pitfalls

Demonstrate the task first with a volunteer for the group so that all the students can see how it works.

Make sure that they sit side by side and have some space to work.

Remind them not to discuss their answers until the end.

When finished discuss which change had the biggest effect on how they felt about the situation. There will be a variety of answers depending on how an individual represents the situation and whether that person is more kinaesthetic, auditory or visual.

Have fun with this. It can prove to be a favourite as the idea of being able to 'shrink and bin' people appeals to young people.

Set them a task to use this strategy away from the classroom and ask them to report back on how they find it next time.

Case studies

Dean (14) came back after this session with a story of how he had used it in French to shrink and bin the teacher who was 'in his face' about his not having done the home-work. He laughed as he told us that he had imagined shrinking her down and then putting her on top of the sports hall roof with her legs dangling down. Asked if he had lost his temper with her as usual he quickly replied 'No, I was too busy imagining.'

When I explain this strategy to young people I put my index finger and thumb together and flick it as if I am shrinking someone. This proved a mistake this time as Ben (14) embellished my small movement. I asked what he had done and he explained that as he found himself getting angry with his Geography teacher he had pushed his chair back, stood up, raised his arm, and held up his thumb and index finger ready to shrink. The teacher had asked him what on earth he thought he was doing, to which Ben replied 'Don't worry Miss, I am just shrinking and binning you.' He was sent out of the classroom. I now usually tell this story along with my small finger movements to issue a word of caution.

Beverly's mum came to see me and asked to know why her daughter appeared less angry. Beverly (15) had told her mum she was filling a skip with all those people she had used the 'shrink and bin' on. Mum was intrigued as to what this strategy was so Beverly taught it to her. Consequently, they shrink and bin each other and the number of confrontations between them has been reduced.

'Bin it ... I am in control'

In this task we need to think of a situation with another person which made us angry and one which we are still angry about.

Choose a partner to work with and sit side by side. Decide who is **A** and who is **B**.

A reads out the statements and questions below exactly as they are written and records the answers in the spaces. **B** answers them. (**A:** Take your time reading out the questions as **B** will need time to think about their answers.)

1. Think of a word to describe the negative emotion you have about a person or situation and score it out of 10. (10 is the strongest.)

   Start score..

2. Is it OK to change this? Or do you need to keep this feeling so that you can learn from it?

   'If you could reduce or remove this negative emotion now, would it be OK?'

   If it is not OK then think of another situation and start again from 1.

3. Now imagine you are watching a DVD of yourself in the situation: let it run through a few times and take a mental note of what you observe.

4. Please answer the following questions about the DVD.

   Can you see yourself in the DVD?...

   Is the DVD in colour or black and white?...

   Is it bright or dim?...

   What size is the picture on the screen?..

   How close is it to you? (Hold up a piece of paper and move it from right on the end of your nose to further away.)..

   Are there any sounds on the DVD?..

   What sort of sounds are they?..

   Are you saying anything to yourself on the inside?...

   Is there any movement in the DVD?..

   Is the movement fast or slow?..

5. Now ask **B** to change each of the qualities of the situation in turn.

Worksheet 5.5 (Cont'd)

For example, turn the DVD from colour to black and white: **'Does the feeling get better? Get worse? Or stay the same? Now what score are you giving it?'**

Repeat the phrase in bold above for each of the qualities you change for them.

Note down what the score is after each change. The aim is to get it down as low as possible. If any scores get worse then simply change them back.

Change 1.............................Score.............................

Change 2.............................Score.............................

Change 3.............................Score.............................

Change 4.............................Score.............................

Change 5.............................Score.............................

Change 6.............................Score.............................

Change 7.............................Score.............................

Change 8.............................Score.............................

Change 9.............................Score.............................

Change 10.............................Score.........................

Start score.............................Final Score..................

Remember that you can have fun with this. For example, what happens if you **imagine** shrinking another person in the situation and then picking them up and putting them in a bin!!!!!!!!!!????????????

Now change over and let your partner read you the statements and questions. Remember to sit side by side.

Photocopiable:

Teacher's notes

Worksheet 5.6: Breathing round the square (5 minutes)

This is a simple strategy for young people to use when they are still at the in-control part of the Anger Path. It works by distracting the brain by giving it something to think about and do, whilst also reaffirming the connection between mind and body thereby helping to lower the heart rate in a stressful situation.

Draw the diagram on flip-chart paper and explain it. Using the worksheet, practise the technique as a group or individually.

Set a task to use this as necessary for the coming week.

Top tips and common pitfalls

Some students will have been told to count to ten when they feel themselves becoming angry and may be sceptical about this. This technique is similar, however, as they have to imagine a square in front of them and then breathe and count their way around it three times, the effect appears to be greater.

Case study

Rebecca (16) had been in a lot of trouble in the past and labelled as 'very angry and dangerous'. I taught her how to do this technique and she now uses it as and when she needs to on a regular basis.

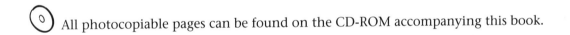 All photocopiable pages can be found on the CD-ROM accompanying this book.

Breathing round the square

This is an easy technique that lets us take control of how we feel. As our mind and body both work together this strategy affects how we feel on the inside which then affects our behaviour. It works by allowing us to deliberately take control of our breathing pattern so we can distract our caveman brain.

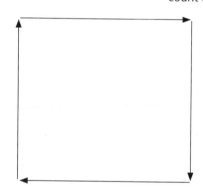

2. Hold that breath for a count of 5

3. Breathe out for a count of 5

1. Breathe in for a count of 5

4. Get ready to start again

Do this three times.

How does this make you feel?

When might you be able to use this? And where?

Photocopiable:

The Behaviour Management Toolkit © Chris Parry-Mitchell, 2012 (SAGE)

6

Lights, action, drama!
Understanding unhelpful roles
and identities

This session introduces the concept of the Drama Triangle developed by Stephen Karpman. The Drama Triangle Diagram was devised as a way of understanding the sometimes repeating patterns of behaviour which occur in our interactions with other people. It is used in this setting to allow the young people to examine their relationships with others in different scenarios and to encourage them to take responsibility for their actions rather than blame others for the situations they find themselves in.

The session starts with a repeated task that allows students to recognise the successes they have had since the last session and to also discuss those aspects of their behaviour that have been less successful. A series of tasks then follows which allows them to explore and understand the Drama Triangle. Having an understanding of the different roles on the triangle allows young people to become more self-regulating and assertive in their behaviour rather than aggressive.

Worksheet 6.1:   What has gone well this week? (20 minutes)

Worksheet 6.2:   Unpicking the drama triangle (45 minutes)

Worksheet 6.3:   Who is who in the drama (30 minutes)

Timings are a guide for discussions and the completion of the relevant worksheet.

Resources required: photocopies of Worksheets 6.1, 6.2 and 6.3; flip-chart paper; pens; pencils; rulers; paper

Recommended further reading

Berne, E. (1964) *Games People Play*, New York: Grove Press.
Karpman, S. (1968) 'Fairy tales and script dramas', *Transactional Analysis*, 7(26): 39–43.
Stewart, A. and Joines, V. (2002) *TA Today: A New Introduction to Transactional Analysis*, Nottingham and Chapel Hill: Lifespace Publishing.

All of these publications provide further in-depth information about Transactional Analysis.

Teacher's notes

Worksheet 6.1: What has gone well this week? (20 minutes)

This worksheet helps to develop an individual's self-esteem and is done on a weekly basis. It enables the students to reflect on what has happened during the past week.

Individuals who have good self-esteem can notice all the small steps that they have made along the way to achieving a goal. However those who have lower self-esteem rather than noting their own progress will tend to constantly compare themselves to a perceived expert and therefore will never feel they have achieved. This task thus begins to reinforce for the students the positive aspects of their behaviour and allows for praise to be received from the group.

The worksheet is completed by the students individually and once this has been done the written contributions for each section will be discussed as a group, starting with the positive aspects. This allows for praise to be received and some discussion and analysis to occur in a safe environment covering the less positive aspects of their week. Completing this task each session with a group has the effect of ensuring the students are noticing aspects of their life, namely, the small steps, which are going well or are positive and so this helps to develop their self-esteem.

Once discussed, the students must select one example from the top of their worksheet and illustrate it. This is then used on a wallchart with their name attached which follows their progress over the rest of the sessions.

Top tips and common pitfalls

Students are not always good at writing down what has gone well and may need some prompting. I usually give them a few examples verbally of the things they could write down and this seems to encourage them to think of other things. For example, 'arrived at school on time, stayed in lessons, remembered equipment or sports kit'.

Some students for whatever reason will have difficult weeks and when this happens ask them to think of anything that has gone well, from speaking politely to just one person (even if it is you), to making a parent a cup of coffee or keeping their room tidy.

What has gone well this week?

Name:

Thinking about this last week at school and at home list three things that have '**gone well**'. ☺☺☺

Possible ideas: you had a good lesson/day; you completed some work in class; you completed some homework; you spoke politely to people; you have been on time ...

1.

2.

3.

Choose your best one from these three and draw it on a piece of paper.

Now write down any things that 'haven't gone as well' this week. ☺☹☺

1.

2.

3.

Pay close attention to the students when they are filling in the worksheet so that you can prompt and assist those who may be struggling.

When the students read out their examples to the group remind them of the ground rules and enforce these as necessary.

Praise, clap, cheer as appropriate for all the positive things they note down!

Ask the group for verbal feedback as appropriate on the less positive aspects of the week. Keep the discussion on this part of the worksheet moving so it doesn't become competitive, namely, on whose behaviour has been the worst. The students will attempt to justify their behaviour so keep your feedback to them non-judgemental and evidence-based if possible.

Teacher's notes

Worksheet 6.2: Unpicking the drama triangle (45minutes)

This worksheet introduces Stephen Karpman's Drama Triangle Diagram as it appeared in 1968 as 'Fairy tales and script drama' in *Transactional Analysis*. He holds that whenever people are playing games when interacting they will step into one of the three roles on the triangle; the Persecutor, the Rescuer, or the Victim. The arrows on the triangle indicate that these positions are interchangeable depending on how the interaction develops.

The Persecutor takes the role of one who puts others down and is out (in teenage speak) 'to get you'. The Rescuer takes the role of offering help and support, whilst the Victim feels 'not OK' and powerless. Each of the roles will the other two in some way.

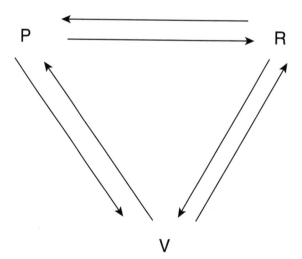

Figure 6.1   The Drama Triangle Diagram (reproduced with kind permission from Stephen Karpman)

Allowing the students to understand this diagram enables them to begin to take responsibility for some of their actions and hopefully by being aware of these they can avoid situations which may leave them feeling unhappy. Young people will invariably tell stories of how bad things are for them, whether that is at home with the adults there or at school with other grown-ups. The Drama Triangle allows them to put some perspective on their situation and creates a level of assertiveness and less of a feeling of powerlessness.

Draw the Drama Triangle on flip-chart paper as it appears on the previous page, with the Victim pointing down. Read through the worksheets explaining the roles and discussing these as necessary. Allow the students plenty of time to think about Drama Triangle situations in various scenarios and then complete the worksheet.

Use the diagram to police any future stories they give about circumstances involving others.

Top tips and common pitfalls

I use a story example to explain the diagram and usually refer to something the young people have told me. For example, a girl (Victim) who told me how awful her teacher was (Persecutor) for giving her a detention after school for being late and how her mum (Rescuer) had rung the school to say that her daughter would not be doing the detention.

Young people respond well to the Drama Triangle diagram and will quickly give you the names of Persecutors and Rescuers in their lives. As they explain, remember to remind them that if that is the case they are playing Victim and that also at some point in the scenario they describe they will have swapped roles.

Insist that once they have learnt and understood this that they stop making Victim-type statements when they relate a situation. This encourages them to accept responsibility for their actions. Some of them can find this very difficult initially as they are using patterns of behaviour which have worked and made sense to them for a long time and it is much easier to blame others around them rather than accept that they have played a part.

Watch out for Rescuers in a group situation; they will be the ones who will save others from making a mistake when perhaps they haven't been listening.

Play 'I Spy the Drama Triangle' in future discussions. This reworking of the children's game allows young people to become more familiar with the Triangle in real-life interactions. As the group discussions continue, anyone who spots a Persecutor-, Rescuer- or Victim-type statement must call attention to it.

Unpicking the Drama Triangle

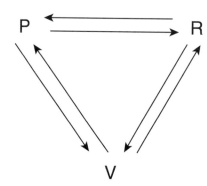

There are three main roles on the drama triangle developed by Stephen Karpman in 1968:

PERSECUTOR: 'You always do that! Why don't you listen? You are useless', or they may just suggest these things but not actually say them. They do not value the others.

RESCUER: 'Here, let me help, I'll sort it out for you. What do you want me to do? I will do it'. They are here to save the VICTIM from the PERSECUTOR. They do not think that others can do things for themselves.

VICTIM: 'It wasn't my fault! I didn't do it! I couldn't help it! It's always me'. Imagine them putting their hand across their head and saying 'Poor me!' They are being 'got' at by the person who is the PERSECUTOR. They do not value themselves and see themselves as powerless in the situation.

As the situation develops, it is usual for there to be some role swapping. We can move from VICTIM to PERSECUTOR, etc., as the DRAMA unfolds.

Below is a very simple example of the Drama Triangle in play:

Dad says to his son '*Why haven't you done your Geography homework? You always leave it to the last minute, it's not good enough!*'

Son says '*It's not my fault, I can't do it.*'

Mum says '*Oh, I didn't realise you couldn't do it, let me help."*

Can you spot who is playing each part?

All of us at some time will play the VICTIM, PERSECUTOR or RESCUER and sometimes we will be dragged into other people's DRAMAs.

Have you sometimes told a friend how you have been picked on or told off by a teacher? If you have been playing the VICTIM you would be looking to your friend to play the RESCUER and make you feel better about the situation. Do you sometimes say horrid things to a younger brother or sister? If you have you have been playing the PERSECUTOR and they were the VICTIM, who rescued them?

Think of some situations when the DRAMA TRIANGLE is in play. At school? At home? With friends?

School:

Home:

With friends:

Case studies

In every session Dominic (13) would tell us in great detail of how the teachers at his school were victimising him from the moment he arrived: he was late; his uniform was incorrect; he had the wrong equipment; he hadn't done his work, etc. Every week we would all listen to this and Jayne (14) would nod sympathetically and offer him suggestions which would help, like texting him when it was time to get up. After completing these worksheets she looked at him and said 'Right, have you got that? I am not rescuing you any more. You need to man up and get on with it.' We all looked at Dominic, waiting for his response, but he just shrugged and said 'OK, I get it; it's up to me.' This was a surreal moment and one which had us all laughing.

Diane (8) learnt about the Drama Triangle and then went on to chastise her older brother Liam (13) about it. Every time he complained about something she could be heard repeating his complaint followed by the words 'Poor Me! Poor Me! I am a help-less Victim.' Teach this along with a cautionary word about using it appropriately or arguments could ensue.

Teacher's notes

Worksheet 6.3: Who is who in the drama? (30 minutes)

This worksheet enables the young people to develop their understanding of the different roles on Stephen Karpman's Drama Triangle by establishing some of the characteristics of each. Students can easily switch from role to role depending on who they are with, the situation they are in, and their past preferences. It is therefore useful for them to gain some insight into the differing thoughts, feelings and behaviours attached to the Persecutor, Rescuer and Victim positions.

Draw a circle on the flip-chart paper with the three section headings on so that the principle of the task can be discussed first. Read through the worksheet and then allow the students to draw three identical circles divided into three equal sections and labelled as those on the worksheet. One circle is for the Persecutor, one for the Rescuer, and one for the Victim. They must then add on to each circle what they think they would be saying to themselves, what they would be feeling, and how they would be behaving whilst in each of the roles of the Drama Triangle. Once they have completed each circle discuss with them which they found the easiest to complete and why: then ask them to share the content of their work.

These can be displayed afterwards as they will provide a useful reference for other sessions. This worksheet can also lead on to discussions about how to avoid the Drama Triangle by accepting responsibility for one's actions, avoiding personal criticism of others, and respecting other's ability to do things for themselves.

Who is who in the DRAMA?

Use this model to find out about the characteristics of each of the roles on the Drama Triangle Diagram devised by Stephen Karpman.

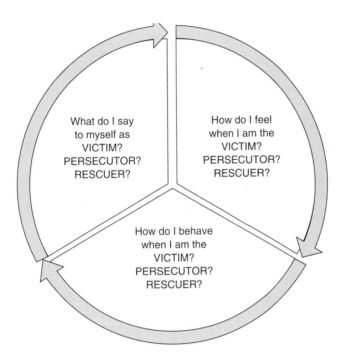

What do I say to myself as VICTIM? PERSECUTOR? RESCUER?

How do I feel when I am the VICTIM? PERSECUTOR? RESCUER?

How do I behave when I am the VICTIM? PERSECUTOR? RESCUER?

Draw three circles; one for the VICTIM, one for the PERSECUTOR, and one for the RESCUER. Use the above model to fill in the characteristics of each in terms of feeling, behaving and saying.

Now compare these. What are the main differences?

Did you end up playing one role more often? In which situations?

Now that you understand the DRAMA TRIANGLE ... watch out for it!!!

Top tips and common pitfalls

This can be a task that the group will complete in pairs if they feel happier doing so.

Discuss each circle as it is completed.

Do not pass judgement on what they have written, especially the comments in the 'What do I say to myself?' box.

Join in when the discussion moves on to which role they find themselves playing more often. I explain that when I am teaching or in parent mode I can naturally play Rescuer and have to stop myself from overdoing it; however, when I am with friends and I feel hard done by I can step into being the Victim. The idea is that the students will develop an understanding of the interchangeable nature of the roles and become more adept at spotting when they step into one of these.

Note that their life experiences to date will influence which role they feel safest in and that may need careful handling.

They will find completing the Victim and Persecutor circles the easiest and may need more guidance with that of Rescuer.

Case studies

I put Natasha (15) and Stuart (15) together to complete this task. She had adopted through experience the role of Persecutor in many interactions whilst Stuart preferred Victim. As they worked together, you could see their individual awareness of each other increase. Up until this point they had been happy in their chosen roles and to be suddenly confronted with an alternative view was interesting.

All photocopiable pages can be found on the CD-ROM accompanying this book.

7

Fast forward: raising aspirations and creating a future

This session is aimed at motivating students to think about their future goals and plans by giving them an understanding of the concept of time and how it impacts on us.

Many young people who are not thriving within education will have a preference for things that happen in the here and now and little awareness of the longer-term consequences of their actions or any real plans for their futures. This task is therefore vital in motivating them for the future and enabling them to see time as linear.

The session starts with a repeated task which allows students to recognise the successes they have had since the last session and also discusses those aspects of their behaviour which have been less successful. A revision task can then be completed, if appropriate, which will allow them to realise how much they have actually covered and learnt about during the sessions. The next worksheet allows them to move themselves forward into the future and make decisions about where they want to be, whilst also making sure that they acknowledge the smaller steps they will have taken to get there.

Worksheet 7.1: What has gone well this week? (20 minutes)

Worksheet 7.2: How much do I know? ... Tons! (45 minutes)

Worksheet 7.3: Fast forward (45 minutes)

Timings are a guide for discussions and the completion of the relevant worksheet.

Resources required: photocopies of Worksheets 7.1, 7.2, and 7.3; flip-chart paper; pens; pencils; felt pens; rulers; cut lengths of lining paper

Teacher's notes

Worksheet 7.1: What has gone well this week? (20 minutes)

This worksheet helps to develop an individual's self-esteem and is done on a weekly basis. It enables the students to reflect on what has happened during the past week.

Individuals who have good self-esteem can notice all the small steps that they have made along the way to achieving a goal. However those who have lower self-esteem rather than noting their own progress will tend to constantly compare themselves to a perceived expert and therefore will never feel they have achieved. This task thus begins to reinforce for the students the positive aspects of their behaviour and allows for praise to be received from the group.

The worksheet is completed by the students individually and once this has been done the written contributions for each section will be discussed as a group, starting with the positive aspects. This allows for praise to be received and some discussion and analysis to occur in a safe environment covering the less positive aspects of their week. Completing this task each session with a group has the effect of ensuring the students are noticing aspects of their life, namely, the small steps, which are going well or are positive and so this helps to develop their self-esteem.

Once discussed, the students must select one example from the top of their worksheet and illustrate it. This is then used on a wallchart with their name attached which follows their progress over the rest of the sessions.

Top tips and common pitfalls

Students are not always good at writing down what has gone well and may need some prompting. I usually give them a few examples verbally of the things they could write down and this seems to encourage them to think of other things. For example, 'arrived at school on time, stayed in lessons, remembered equipment or sports kit'.

Some students for whatever reason will have difficult weeks and when this happens ask them to think of anything that has gone well, from speaking politely to just one person (even if it is you), to making a parent a cup of coffee or keeping their room tidy.

Pay close attention to the students when they are filling in the worksheet so that you can prompt and assist those who may be struggling.

When the students read out their examples to the group remind them of the ground rules and enforce these as necessary.

Praise, clap, cheer as appropriate for all the positive things they note down!

Ask the group for verbal feedback as appropriate on the less positive aspects of the week. Keep the discussion on this part of the worksheet moving so it doesn't become competitive, namely, on whose behaviour has been the worst. The students will attempt to justify their behaviour so keep your feedback to them non-judgemental and evidence-based if possible.

What has gone well this week?

Name:

Thinking about this last week at school and at home list three things that have **'gone well'**. ☺☺☺

Possible ideas: you had a good lesson/day; you completed some work in class; you completed some homework; you spoke politely to people; you have been on time ...

1.

2.

3.

Choose your best one from these three and draw it on a piece of paper.

Now write down any things that 'haven't gone as well' this week. ☺☹☺

1.

2.

3.

Photocopiable:

The Behaviour Management Toolkit © Chris Parry-Mitchell, 2012 (SAGE)

Teacher's notes

Worksheet 7.2: How much do I know? ... Tons! (45 minutes)

This is a revision task which allows the students to recognise how much they have covered and now have an understanding of.

Initially they will need to list the content on the worksheet and then feedback on which bits they have found most useful to them.

Once the list has been discussed and confirmed, the students can create their own diagrammatic account of the content on a divided-up piece of paper, putting one model, idea or strategy into each of the boxes.

They can then keep the picture format as a handy reminder for future reference.

Top tips and common pitfalls

Make sure that they write the list on their own initially.

Use previous flip charts to remind them of what has been covered earlier.

Offer a treat for the most colourful and detailed revision poster.

Laminate these as they are then more likely to keep them!

Case study

Alec (14) has kept his revision poster in his planner two years after creating it. He says that when he is fed up he can get this out and remember doing all of the work.

Teacher's notes

Worksheet 7.3: Fast forward (45 minutes)

This worksheet is completed with the aim of creating a motivating future plan for the students. This technique was created by the NLP founders John Bandler and Richard Grinder in the 1970s when they modelled excellence in others. They noted that those who were successful in being motivated towards and achieving their goals saw time differently from those who did not. As human beings we presume that others see time and store memories in a similar way to ourselves. That is, however, debatable and there are in fact two common ways in which we do this along with a host of variations.

Start by discussing with the students what they understand by the word 'time' and record their answers on flip-chart paper.

How much do I know? ... Tons!

As we are half-way through the programme let's recap on what we have done.

List as many things as you can remember..............

What have you used? Did it work?

Draw everything you have learnt on the folded piece of paper: you can now keep this as a reminder.

Thinking of the goal you set on the POSSE ... how are you doing?

What else do you think you will need help with in the coming weeks?

Photocopiable:
The Behaviour Management Toolkit © Chris Parry-Mitchell, 2012 (SAGE)

Then read out the following script slowly to the students, asking them to close their eyes first. Pause in between each phrase so that they have enough time to visualise and think about what you are asking them. This allows both you and them to understand how they store memories in their heads and how they see time.

> Close your eyes. Now think of a hobby or pastime that you enjoy doing regularly ... Imagine doing that hobby/pastime a year ago ... now imagine doing that hobby/pastime six months ago ... now imagine doing that hobby/pastime three months ago ... now imagine doing that hobby/pastime last month ... now imagine doing that hobby/pastime two weeks ago ... now imagine doing that hobby/pastime a week ago ... now imagine doing that hobby/pastime yesterday ... now imagine doing that hobby/pastime today ... now imagine doing that hobby/pastime tomorrow ... now imagine doing that hobby/pastime next week ... now imagine doing that hobby/pastime in two weeks' time ... now imagine doing that hobby/pastime in a month's time ... now imagine doing that hobby/pastime in three months' time ... now imagine doing that hobby/pastime in six months' time ... now imagine doing that hobby/pastime at this time next year ... now keeping your eyes shut and knowing that you will be right, point in the direction that you think doing your hobby/pastime last year is ... and keeping your eyes shut and knowing that you will be right, point in the direction that you think doing your hobby/pastime in the future is ... keeping your arms where they are ... open your eyes.

At this point the students will be pointing in various directions, but there will be two positions which will probably be more common than the rest and these are drawn below.

Future ——————— Present ——————— Past

The past will be to the left and the future to the right: this is called a 'through time preference'. Alternatively:

Past

Present

Future

Here the past will be behind the student and the future in front: this is called an 'in time preference'.

Neither is better than the other as each has its benefits. Those with a through time preference will typically be punctual, good at planning and learning from mistakes, yet not always great at relaxing and getting lost in the moment. On the other hand those with an in time preference will be great at relaxing and getting lost in the moment but may not be overly punctual, good at learning from previous mistakes, or well-versed in planning for a future.

Understanding this concept ensures that young people can take more control of time and plan out their lives accordingly instead of letting things happen to them and then wondering how this came to pass.

Give each student a large piece of lining paper and follow the instructions on Worksheet 7.3.

Work through the task, ensuring all of the students have plenty of detail about their fantastic future. As they complete this, note that the tense used on the worksheet changes. When they have detailed their future they will need to look back at themselves now and list the things they *did* to get to their future. This is a language pattern which presumes they have been successful and it is a vital trick for ensuring they will create a motivating and successful future.

Display the finished fantastic futures on the wall so each student is reminded visually of their plan.

Top tips and common pitfalls

Read out the passage slowly and give students enough time to understand what they are doing. Before reading I will always ask, 'How many of you think that everyone does time in their head in the same way?' Then I will suggest we carry out an experiment to see if we do the same and give an overview of what is expected of them before I ask them to close their eyes.

A few will not understand and may need some of the details repeated before being asked to open their eyes.

Reassure them that they are safe whilst they close their eyes and nothing strange is going to happen.

Have fun discussing the two preferences. I usually tell them my preference through time and explain how that affects me when: for example, how on holiday I am constantly thinking of what needs to be done when I get home and that I have a friend who is never on time so I will tell her I will pick her up at 7.30pm and not get there until 8pm as by doing that there is a better chance she will be ready!

When completing the worksheet, ensure they include lots of details and add comments like 'Well done' when they get to key points like passing examinations.

Do not be shocked by what they put down. However, do encourage realism whilst also gently raising their aspirations.

Remember to use the *past tense* when talking to them about what they *did*. This may feel unfamiliar at the start yet it is an essential feature.

Some may go further into the future than just the five years. That is acceptable, so let them do it.

Fast forward

Where do you want to be in the future? What do you want to be doing?

1. Draw a line along the bottom of a large piece of paper and draw 'you' on the left-hand side as you are now. What is going on for you now? What are you doing?

2. Draw 'you' in five years' time on the right-hand side. What are you doing? Where are you living? What is going on for you now? This is your 'FANTASTIC FUTURE' where anything is possible, so think BIG!

   Me now   Me in five years' time

3. Now think about your 'Fantastic Future' look back at 'today' and decide: 'What were all the key things I did to get to my 'Fantastic Future?'

   The first thing I did was...............

   Next I did...........................

   Next I did...........................

   Next I did...........................

   Next I did...........................

   Next I did...........................

   Finally I did.........................

   Add as many 'Next I did' statements as you want: indeed the more the better, as you will then have lots of detail.

   Check that you have everything you did written down.

4. Add all of these details to your picture by writing them down and then adding a drawing. Start with what you did first and then work your way to the future.

5. Make sure you have it all and everything is in the correct order. For example, when did you learn to drive? What grades did you get in your exams? What did people say to you when you did so well? How did you feel?

6. Put this on the wall and keep it safe: it is your path to your 'FANTASTIC FUTURE'.

Photocopiable:

The Behaviour Management Toolkit © Chris Parry-Mitchell, 2012 (SAGE)

Case studies

Natalie (14) completed her fantastic future and called me over to read it. On it she had put the usual things apart from one, 'Aged 19 boob job!' Shocking as this may appear, this was her reality.

Whilst observing Damien (16) putting the finishing touches to his work I noticed that he had drawn three children and asked for some clarification. He quickly replied with 'Well to get a house you need kids!'

Comments like these make me sad, as I realise how many young people have low aspirations and are committed to prophecy they believe they have been given.

Seb (14) completed his work indicating that he wanted to study Sport and Law. He is now well on his way to doing that and high grades have been predicted for him in both subjects.

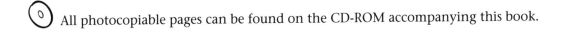 All photocopiable pages can be found on the CD-ROM accompanying this book.

8

Step over here: developing an understanding of the views of others

This session aims to introduce the idea that to gain wisdom in any situation we need the ability to look at it from the perspective of different people. Young people tend to see things only from their perspective and can get quite entrenched in that position, doing all they can to defend and justify their behaviour. Some will also hold unhelpful identities about themselves and therefore it is important that they recognise this fact and begin to change this view.

The session starts with a repeated task which allows students to recognise the successes they have had since the last session and also discusses those aspects of their behaviour which have been less successful. The tasks that follow allow them to first examine how a situation or relationship with another person could be different from different perspectives and then to look at their own and other people's opinions about themselves.

Worksheet 8.1: What has gone well this week? (20 minutes)

Worksheet 8.2: Step over here (45 minutes)

Worksheet 8.3: Me, myself, you and I (30 minutes)

Timings are a guide for discussion and completion of the relevant worksheet.

Resources required: photocopies of Worksheets 8.1, 8.2 and 8.3; flip-chart paper; pens; pencils; rulers; paper

Teacher's notes

Worksheet 8.1: What has gone well this week? (20 minutes)

This worksheet helps to develop an individual's self-esteem and is done on a weekly basis. It enables the students to reflect on what has happened during the past week.

Individuals who have good self-esteem can notice all the small steps that they have made along the way to achieving a goal. However those who have lower self-esteem rather than noting their own progress will tend to constantly compare themselves to a perceived expert and therefore will never feel they have achieved. This task thus begins to reinforce for the students the positive aspects of their behaviour and allows for praise to be received from the group.

The worksheet is completed by the students individually and once this has been done the written contributions for each section will be discussed as a group, starting with the positive aspects. This allows for praise to be received and some discussion and analysis to occur in a safe environment covering the less positive aspects of their week. Completing this task each session with a group has the effect of ensuring the students are noticing aspects of their life, namely, the small steps, which are going well or are positive and so this helps to develop their self-esteem.

Once discussed, the students must select one example from the top of their worksheet and illustrate it. This is then used on a wallchart with their name attached which follows their progress over the rest of the sessions.

Top tips and common pitfalls

Students are not always good at writing down what has gone well and may need some prompting. I usually give them a few examples verbally of the things they could write down and this seems to encourage them to think of other things. For example, 'arrived at school on time, stayed in lessons, remembered equipment or sports kit'.

Some students for whatever reason will have difficult weeks and when this happens ask them to think of anything that has gone well, from speaking politely to just one person (even if it is you), to making a parent a cup of coffee or keeping their room tidy.

Pay close attention to the students when they are filling in the worksheet so that you can prompt and assist those who may be struggling.

When the students read out their examples to the group remind them of the ground rules and enforce these as necessary.

Praise, clap, cheer as appropriate for all the positive things they note down!

Ask the group for verbal feedback as appropriate on the less positive aspects of the week. Keep the discussion on this part of the worksheet moving so it doesn't become competitive, namely, on whose behaviour has been the worst. The students will attempt to justify their behaviour so keep your feedback to them non-judgemental and evidence-based if possible.

What has gone well this week?

Name:

Thinking about this last week at school and at home list three things that have '**gone well**'. ☺☺☺

Possible ideas: you had a good lesson/day; you completed some work in class; you completed some homework; you spoke politely to people; you have been on time ...

1.

2.

3.

Choose your best one from these three and draw it on a piece of paper.

Now write down any things that 'haven't gone as well' this week? ☺☺☺

1.

2.

3.

Photocopiable:
The Behaviour Management Toolkit © Chris Parry-Mitchell, 2012 (SAGE)

Teacher's notes

Worksheet 8.2: Step over here (45 minutes)

This task encourages young people to view situations from other perspectives. It invites them to first step into the shoes of the other person involved and then to disassociate from the situation by taking the position of a wise, detached observer or a fly on the wall. The aim is to provide insight and understanding into their own and other's behaviour so they can see how it impacts on the situation and may lead them to behave differently in the future.

Read through the worksheet. The students must work in pairs and one reads through the worksheet whilst the other silently processes and follows the instructions as they are given.

Part One asks for the student working to imagine the other person in the situation that is in front of them and to notice how it feels and any behaviours, words or voice tones. This is processed silently. Part Two invites the student to step into the shoes of the other person involved and to notice what it is like in the situation with the student, again noting how it feels and any behaviours, words or voice tones. This is also processed silently. Part Three asks the student to step over to the fly on the wall position which is detached from the situation as if they were a wise observer. From here they will be invited to observe the two people in the situation, noticing behaviours, words and voice tones. In this position, they will then be asked what advice could be given to the student in the situation and to process this silently as before. Part Four asks the student to step back to the original position, imagining that the other person is in front of them. However, now they have the advice from the fly on the wall they will be encouraged to notice how that may change or influence the situation for the better.

The pair of students can then change position and work through the process again for their partner to experience it.

Once both have had their turn, they can then discuss their experiences.

An alternative method for completing this task is to treat it as an interview. The student actually answers the questions verbally as these are asked, answering as if the other person in Part Two and as the fly on the wall in Part Three.

Top tips and common pitfalls

This is a powerful experience for young people and one which many will be unfamiliar with, so allow them sufficient time here.

Do not push to find out what they have discovered as sometimes the realisation that they have played a part in how a given situation unfolded can be a reality check and they won't want to share this.

In between each of the parts ask them to move about a bit to shake off any unpleasant feelings.

Make sure that they physically move as they go through the exercise. Name cards can be put on the floor if appropriate.

Ensure that each pair remains silent about what they are doing until both students have completed the task. If they start to discuss the situation it can become an excuse to have a good gossip and a opportunity to receive validation from another.

Young people love doing this task and enjoy the idea of playing somebody else. Let them run with it.

This is usually completed standing up, with the person reading the worksheet standing at the side of the student working and moving with that student as they move.

Step over here

This task allows us to step into someone else's shoes to find out a little more about a situation. It helps us get a different perspective and allows us to behave differently and more assertively in the future.

There are three places to physically move to in this exercise:

- You.

- The other person.

- The fly on the wall, who has nothing to do with the situation and is just a wise observer.

Work with a partner. They will read the following out for you and all you have to do is nod when you are ready to continue with the next part. Keep your findings from this investigation until the end of the exercise and then only share these with your partner if you want to.

Part One:

Close your eyes. Choose a situation with another person you would like to investigate. It can be something that has happened already or something that has yet to happen.

Step into 'YOU' and see the 'OTHER PERSON' in your imagination in front of you.

Notice everything about the 'OTHER PERSON': their body position, facial expression, etc.

Notice what 'YOU' are saying and what the 'OTHER PERSON' is saying: note the words, the tone of voice and the volume.

Notice what 'YOU' are saying to yourself on the inside and how you feel being with the 'OTHER PERSON'.

Notice everything that is significant about the situation.

Nod when you are ready to move on.

Part Two:

Move and step into the position of the 'OTHER PERSON' and see 'YOU' in your imagination.

Notice everything about 'YOU': their body position, facial expression, etc.

Notice what 'YOU' are saying, the voice tone and the volume.

Notice what it feels like to be here with 'YOU'.

Notice everything there is to notice about this situation.

Nod when you are ready to move on.

Part Three:

Move and step into the position of the 'FLY ON THE WALL'. From here you are just an observer of 'YOU' and the 'OTHER PERSON'.

Notice everything about 'YOU' and the 'OTHER PERSON': body positions, facial expressions, etc.

Notice what 'YOU' and the 'OTHER PERSON' are saying, the voice tones and volume.

Notice everything that is significant about 'YOU' and the 'OTHER PERSON'.

From this 'FLY ON THE WALL' position what advice would you give 'YOU' so that they can experience the situation differently? How could they behave differently?

Nod when you are ready to move on.

Part Four:

Move and step back to the position of 'YOU', knowing what you now know from the 'FLY ON THE WALL'.

Let the situation with the 'OTHER PERSON' run through again and notice how it has changed when you behave differently and take on board the advice of the 'FLY ON THE WALL.'

Nod when you have finished.

If you want, you can move and step back in the position of 'OTHER PERSON' to notice how things are different for them also.

Photocopiable:

The Behaviour Management Toolkit © Chris Parry-Mitchell, 2012 (SAGE)

Case studies

John (16) had chronic attendance problems at school. His home situation left him vulnerable and his girlfriend was the only person whom he valued. I completed 'Step over here' with him using his girlfriend as the other person in the situation. He processed everything silently and at the end turned and said 'Well Chris, she thinks I am a lazy you know what!' He had realised that she would probably not find him fun to be with in the long term if all he did was stay in bed all day! His attendance improved and he is now attending a post-16 training course.

Completed as an interview, Lee (13) was constantly being asked to leave the class for poor, often rude behaviour. I decided that we would use 'Step over here' to examine the situation and to prompt him to have a look at his behaviour from the teacher's perspective. We labelled the chairs and set to work. I asked the questions pretending I was a journalist and he answered them verbally. His insight into the situation was very adult. Lee was able to tell me why he felt the need to be rude and behave inappropriately and how both he and the teacher could do things differently to improve the situation. I wrote up the work and then met Lee and the teacher concerned to pass on his insight and to add the details from the teacher's perspective. The teacher concerned was very understanding and open to the suggestions that Lee made; at the very least these had reopened the lines of communication between them. (Remember to put a note on the door when you are working. I forgot to do this and the look on the face of another member of staff who burst in to the room by mistake to see Lee pretending to be the teacher was interesting to say the least!)

Teacher's notes

Worksheet 8.3: Me, myself, you and I (30 minutes)

This task allows the young people to examine some of the labels they give to themselves and those that have been given by others. It is useful to complete this task as it will give staff some insight into the thinking of a young person and perhaps offer reasons for some behaviours.

Read through the worksheet with the students and then ask them to fill in the two sections silently. They may find it easier to start with the labels that are given to them by other people before moving on to list some of the things they say about themselves. Once one side has been completed, discuss what has been written as a group and whether or not the statements are useful and promote a positive identity.

As a development of this task, ask them to select one example from the 'I' list and alter it to produce a more positive statement. Note this down and remind them of it in the future.

Me, myself, you and I

Sometimes the way we talk about ourselves is not useful. And sometimes the way other people talk about us is not useful either.

For example, if I describe myself like this: 'I am so bad at ...' or 'I am useless at ...', or let others label me 'You're hopeless' or 'You are a complete waste of space', then we are suggesting to ourselves that this is all true.

What happens if you don't think of a purple giraffe? Or you don't think of a big piece of chocolate cake? You have to think of them, as your brain hears first ... 'purple giraffe' or 'big piece of chocolate cake' and then it hears ... the *don't* instruction.

List below some of the limiting things that you use to describe yourself and the labels others have given you.

I am   You are

I am not   You are not

I do not   You do not

I ....   You ....

Photocopiable:
The Behaviour Management Toolkit © Chris Parry-Mitchell, 2012 (SAGE)

Top tips and common pitfalls

Don't be shocked or surprised by students' honesty or the labels they may have been given or applied to themselves.

This task may initially produce lists from some saying how fabulous they are. After that they will slowly add in some of the unhelpful labels, so do give them sufficient time.

If the group is working well together and there is trust between the members they will usually share what they have written. Leave those who do not want to contribute their list to the group and speak to them individually afterwards.

Case study

Sophie (14) read out her list very matter of factly: ' I am really thick, I am ugly, I am no good at anything, I don't work hard enough', followed by 'You are a waster, You don't listen, You don't know how to behave'. This was a useful insight on how she thought and felt about events and led to the group of mostly boys being shocked at first and then proceeding to look after her at every opportunity.

 All photocopiable pages can be found on the CD-ROM accompanying this book.

9

Premier skills: skills for successful learners

This session allows students to map out how they are successful learners whilst also introducing them to a strategy they can use to learn things in the future. As human beings we learn new things almost every day and so by completing these tasks the young people will recognise this talent and then build on it.

The session starts with a repeated task which allows students to recognise the successes they have had since the last session and also discusses those aspects of their behaviour which have been less successful. Two tasks then follow, the first of which allows each student to analyse how they learn successfully whilst the second teaches them the basis of the NLP spelling strategy created by Robert Dilts and then developed by Cricket Kemp and Caitlin Walker of Magical Spelling® in 1992.

Worksheet 9.1:   What has gone well this week? (20 minutes)

Worksheet 9.2:   What do I need to learn? (30 minutes)

Worksheet 9.3:   The learning space (45 minutes)

Timings are a guide for discussions and the completion of the relevant worksheet.

Resources required: photocopies of Worksheet 9.1, 9.2, and 9.3; flip-chart paper; pens; pencils; felt pens; rulers

Recommended further reading

www.magicalspellinglimited.com and www.trainingattention.co.uk. Both of these websites provide information on systemic modelling and creating learning spaces.

Teacher's notes

Worksheet 9.1: What has gone well this week? (20 minutes)

This worksheet helps to develop an individual's self-esteem and is done on a weekly basis. It enables the students to reflect on what has happened during the past week.

Individuals who have good self-esteem can notice all the small steps that they have made along the way to achieving a goal. However those who have lower self-esteem rather than noting their own progress will tend to constantly compare themselves to a perceived expert and therefore will never feel they have achieved. This task thus begins to reinforce for the students the positive aspects of their behaviour and allows for praise to be received from the group.

The worksheet is completed by the students individually and once this has been done the written contributions to each section will be discussed as a group, starting with the positive aspects. This allows for praise to be received and some discussion and analysis to occur in a safe environment covering the less positive aspects of their week. Completing this task each session with a group has the effect of ensuring the students are noticing aspects of their life, namely, the small steps, which are going well or are positive and so this helps to develop their self-esteem.

Once discussed, the students must select one example from the top of their worksheet and illustrate it. This is then used on a wallchart with their name attached which follows their progress over the rest of the sessions.

Top tips and common pitfalls

Students are not always good at writing down what has gone well and may need some prompting. I usually give them a few examples verbally of the things they could write down and this seems to encourage them to think of other things. For example, 'arrived at school on time, stayed in lessons, remembered equipment or sports kit'.

Some students for whatever reason will have difficult weeks and when this happens ask them to think of anything that has gone well, from speaking politely to just one person (even if it is you), to making a parent a cup of coffee or keeping their room tidy.

Pay close attention to the students when they are filling in the worksheet so that you can prompt and assist those who may be struggling.

When the students read out their examples to the group remind them of the ground rules and enforce these as necessary.

Praise, clap, cheer as appropriate for all the positive things they note down!

Ask the group for verbal feedback as appropriate on the less positive aspects of the week. Keep the discussion on this part of the worksheet moving so it doesn't become competitive, namely, on whose behaviour has been the worst. The students will attempt to justify their behaviour so keep your feedback to them non-judgemental and evidence-based if possible.

What has gone well this week?

Name:

Thinking about this last week at school and at home list three things that have **'gone well'**. ☺☺☺

Possible ideas: you had a good lesson/day; you completed some work in class; you completed some homework; you spoke politely to people, you have been on time ...

1.

2.

3.

Choose your best one from these three and draw it on a piece of paper.

Now write down any things that 'haven't gone as well' this week. ☺☹☺

1.

2.

3.

Photocopiable:

The Behaviour Management Toolkit © Chris Parry-Mitchell, 2012 (SAGE)

Teacher's notes

Worksheet 9.2: What do I need to learn? (30 minutes)

This task allows students to model what it is they actually do when they are learning to the best of their ability. It is beneficial for them to do so as it enables them to self-regulate in the future or adapt one of the components so that they are better placed to learn.

Ask them to think of a really good lesson or one which they enjoy doing. They must then complete the worksheet by adding their own details to the three sections. In the thinking section they should list anything they say to themselves when they are having a positive learning experience; in the feeling section they should write down how they feel when they are learning in this way; in the behaving section they should add all the behaviours that someone else would notice and then be able to confirm that they were indeed learning at their best.

Discuss what has been written after each section has been completed.

When this has been completed ask them to give a metaphor for what they are like when they are learning well. Discuss how these can be useful to them.

To develop this further, the same format can be adopted to map out other states (e.g. relaxation, anger, confidence etc.).

Top tips and common pitfalls

Depending on the group, it may be easier to start with the behaviour section as this is something others will see as evidence and is more concrete for the students to write about.

Display the diagrams and draw attention to these, using the behaviour section to give feedback to the students about what you may or may not be observing as they learn.

Use some of the examples on the wall to encourage them to create a metaphor. I usually suggest that learning at their best may be like dozing off to sleep after a large lunch. This will prompt a 'No it doesn't', which can be followed up quickly with a 'So what's it like then?' Sponges, Vacuum Cleaners, Butterflies, Water disappearing down a Plug and Astronauts in Space are a few of the examples received.

Case study

Megan (11) created a colourful and detailed diagram of herself learning well. I had it photocopied for her so that she could take it into school and share it with her teachers. They could then use it as a way of keeping her on track in lessons.

What do I need to learn?

When I am learning I am like ....

Complete the diagram by adding what you think, what you feel, and how you behave when you are learning well.

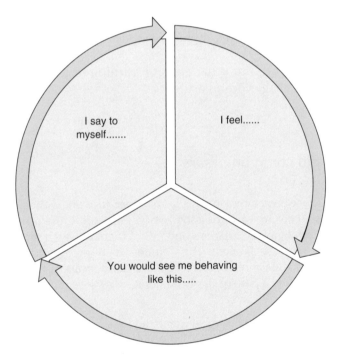

Teacher's notes

Worksheet 9.3: My learning space (45 minutes)

This worksheet teaches the young people about a concept created by Robert Dilts and then further developed by Cricket Kemp and Caitlin Walker of Magical Spelling® in 1988. It works from an understanding that as human beings we learn by storing visually remembered pictures in our brains. The direction in which our eyes go when we process a question relating to a visual image is an indication of which side we store these on. It will usually be up and to the left for most people, but occasionally it can be up and to the right. Young people will sometimes have a view of themselves as poor learners and this can lead them to underachieving in many areas. They can also make unconscious connections between believing they are a poor speller to believing they will therefore be a poor reader and learner. Teaching them about this enables them to have success and begins to break down any barriers to learning that they may have created in an effort to protect themselves from failure.

The worksheet starts with the students working in pairs and asking each other the questions listed so that they can determine which direction their eyes move. Once this has been done they can move on to follow the process as outlined by bullet points.

This can be developed into other areas of learning (e.g. scientific equations, times tables, foreign language vocabulary, etc.).

Top tips and common pitfalls

I start this worksheet by asking for a volunteer to work with. Once one has been selected I ask them to leave the room whilst I explain to the others that I am going to ask that student a few questions and I want them to watch their eyes to see if they go up to the left or to the right. The volunteer then returns and I ask them questions which require a visually remembered picture to be recalled. The rest of the students observe silently until a pattern has been noted. They love doing this and will probably clamour to be next.

Choose who works with whom and watch out for any students who are clearly anxious about the process. Staff should work with them instead.

In general let the students choose their own words; they will know the level they are at. Check that all the words are spelt correctly before they begin.

Young people who are anxious about spelling are not accessing the part of the brain that is necessary for learning. Distract them by having a detailed conversation with them about whatever it is they enjoy doing; only when you see them visibly relax should you hold up the word.

This can be a very positive experience for the young people and they may be surprised how easy it is. They could start challenging each other to spell longer and longer words. Keep a check on this.

Make sure that the person holding the word is standing up.

Ensure that they have a quiet space in which to carry out the process.

Worksheet 9.3

My learning space

All of us store images in our head of the things we have done, seen and learnt. Think about what you did last night. Can you get a picture of it in your head?

Stand opposite a partner, who is sitting down, ask them the following questions and as you do so notice their eye movements.

- What colour is your front door?

- What pictures do you have on the walls of your bedroom?

- How do I get from the kitchen to the bathroom in your house?

- What colour is your toothbrush?

- Describe what you can see out of your bedroom window.

Keep looking at your partner and notice where their eyes go as they get the answer. Ask them similar questions until you find their pattern. Their eyes will usually move up to the left or up to the right.

My partner's eyes go...

My eyes go..

This is the place where you store your visually remembered images and this is the place you can put all the new things you will learn and need to remember in the future.

My learning space

This process is based on Magical Spelling.®

- Select a word you have difficulty spelling.

- Think of something you really enjoy doing and get a clear picture of it in your head and a good feeling about doing it.

- Ask your partner to write the word down in small letters (make sure it is spelt correctly).

- Ask your partner to hold the word up, level with where your eyes went; they will need to stand up to get it in just the right place.

- Let your eyes drift up to the word (just your eyes) and think of the thing you really enjoy doing and how good that feels.

- Tell your partner about what you enjoy doing as they hold up the word.

- Ask your partner to cover the word with another piece of paper and then uncover it again. Do this a few times whilst you still think of the thing you enjoy doing.

- When you are ready write down the word and check if you have spelt it correctly. Give yourself a cheer.

- When you have done this say the word out loud, letter by letter: forwards first and then backwards.

- Remember to keep moving your eyes upwards to your learning space to check it out as that is where you have stored it.

When you can spell a word in both directions you have obviously learnt it and have a visually remembered picture of the word. Now help your partner to put a word in their learning space.

Case studies

Ashleigh (12) learnt this quickly and easily. The following week she asked if she could tell the group a story. She explained that her brother who was 8 had learning difficulties and struggled to spell his name and other words. Ashleigh had gone home and taught her brother the process; checking out his eye movement, asking him to think of playing football and then holding up his forename on a piece of paper. He had easily learnt it and gone on then to spell his surname and other words she selected. Ashleigh's Mum rang to thank me and told me they were now learning three words a night with him. To hear Ashleigh explain what she had gone home and done was a privilege.

Gary (14) hated reading out loud and became aggressive if pushed. A discussion with him when he was calmer revealed his beliefs: 'I can't spell so I can't read so I am not very clever.' This shocked me. After some persuasion he agreed to give the process a chance. Distracted by thinking about playing football he quickly spelt the words on the paper, surprising himself in the process. He was consequently moved up a set in English and has gone from strength to strength. His belief in himself had changed.

 All photocopiable pages can be found on the CD-ROM accompanying this book.

10

Look at me now ... bring it on! Reflection and skills for the future

This session closes the group whilst also allowing the young people to note the progress they have made. It also introduces a visualisation technique which they can use at any time in their lives to feel better about an event or situation. It is important when working in this way with young people that they complete the work feeling positive and also supported for their futures.

The session starts with a repeated task which allows students to recognise the successes they have had since the last session and also discusses those aspects of their behaviour which have been less successful. The next task is a simple visualisation technique which will be beneficial to them in the future. The final task allows them to reflect on their journey through the work whilst also acknowledging where they started.

Worksheet 10.1:   What has gone well this week? (20 minutes)

Worksheet 10.2:   The Bring It On Circle (20 minutes)

Worksheet 10.3:   The upgraded Ferrari (45 minutes)

Timings are a guide for discussions and the completion of the relevant worksheet.

Resources required: photocopies of Worksheets 10.1, 10.2, and 10.3; flip-chart paper; paper; pens; pencils; felt pens; rulers

Teacher's notes

Worksheet 10.1: What has gone well this week? (20 minutes)

This worksheet helps to develop an individual's self-esteem and is done on a weekly basis. It enables the students to reflect on what has happened during the past week.

Individuals who have good self-esteem can notice all the small steps that they have made along the way to achieving a goal. However those who have lower self-esteem rather than noting their own progress will tend to constantly compare themselves to a perceived expert and therefore will never feel they have achieved. This task thus begins to reinforce for the students the positive aspects of their behaviour and allows for praise to be received from the group.

The worksheet is completed by the students individually and once this has been done the written contributions to each section will be discussed as a group, starting with the positive aspects. This allows for praise to be received and some discussion and analysis to occur in a safe environment covering the less positive aspects of their week. Completing this task each session with a group has the effect of ensuring the students are noticing aspects of their life, namely, the small steps, which are going well or are positive and so this helps to develop their self-esteem.

Once discussed, the students must select one example from the top of their worksheet and illustrate it. This is then used on a wallchart with their name attached which follows their progress over the rest of the sessions.

Top tips and common pitfalls

Students are not always good at writing down what has gone well and may need some prompting. I usually give them a few examples verbally of the things they could write down and this seems to encourage them to think of other things. For example, 'arrived at school on time, stayed in lessons, remembered equipment or sports kit'.

Some students for whatever reason will have difficult weeks and when this happens ask them to think of anything that has gone well, from speaking politely to just one person (even if it is you), to making a parent a cup of coffee or keeping their room tidy.

Pay close attention to the students when they are filling in the worksheet so that you can prompt and assist those who may be struggling.

When the students read out their examples to the group remind them of the ground rules and enforce these as necessary.

Praise, clap, cheer as appropriate for all the positive things they note down!

What has gone well this week?

Name:

Thinking about this last week at school and at home list three things that have '**gone well**'. ☺☺☺

Possible ideas: you had a good lesson/day; you completed some work in class; you completed some homework; you spoke politely to people; you have been on time ...

1.

2.

3.

Choose your best one from these three and draw it on a piece of paper.

Now write down any things that 'haven't gone as well' this week. ☺☹☺

1.

2.

3.

Ask the group for verbal feedback as appropriate on the less positive aspects of their week. Keep the discussion on this part of the worksheet moving so it doesn't become competitive, namely, on whose behaviour has been the worst. The students will attempt to justify their behaviour so keep your feedback to them non-judgemental and evidence-based if possible.

Teacher's notes

Worksheet 10.2: The Bring It On Circle (20 minutes)

This task teaches the young people a process which enables them to access a memory and to use the details of it to allow them to feel positive again in the future. Young people can often feel anxious in situations such as interviews or examinations and this strategy allows them to feel more in control. It distracts the part of the brain that is responsible for fight or flight by giving it something constructive to do.

Begin by putting the students into pairs. The student experiencing the process stands up and closes their eyes whilst their partner reads out the worksheet. Once this has been done they need to swap roles. Only when both have finished will they share with each other how they felt the process went and the details concerning their Bring It On Circles.

Students may need to practise this so give them sufficient time to do so.

As a further task, and if appropriate, the students could draw pictures of their Bring It On Circles.

Top tips and common pitfalls

Make sure they do not discuss their circles until each pair has had a chance to experience the process. This means that the process stays clean and one person's opinions and experience do not contaminate another's.

Allow them a quiet space to complete the process. Too many circles close together can lead to hurt feelings if others stand on or in them!

Some students may not be able to access one particular positive memory. Discuss a few situations with them when they have felt comfortable and use these grouped together.

Case study

Katie (17) suffered very badly from examination nerves, so much so that she was physically sick prior to each one. I completed this process with her and she used the Leavers' Ball she had attended as her positive memory. I took her through the process a few times, layering up details each time. She loved the experience. When I saw her a few weeks later she told me that she was using the process by imagining that her desk was sitting in the middle of her Bring It On Circle in the examination room, ready and waiting for her to do her best.

The Bring It On Circle

Work with a partner and ask them to read this out for you. All you have to do is stand up, close your eyes if you want to, and follow the instructions. When you have finished this, swap over.

1. Think of a time when you were feeling good and at your best. Take yourself back to that situation: see what you could see, hear any sounds you could hear, and remember how you felt. Get a really clear picture of this in your head. Nod when you are ready to move on.

2. Let a feeling of confidence and excellence build up. As this happens, imagine there is a circle on the floor around your feet. Notice everything about your circle. Is there a sound that indicates how powerful it is? Nod when you are ready to move on.

3. Let this feeling of confidence and excellence build and build, and as it does, let the circle grow and grow all around you. When the feelings of confidence and excellence are the best they can be, step outside of your circle and leave your 'Bring It On' feelings inside it.

4. Now think of a time/situation in the future when you will want your 'Bring It On' feelings. See and hear what will be there *just before* you want them.

5. When you have the *just before* clear in your mind, step back into your circle and feel those 'Bring It On' feelings again. Now imagine the future situation happening around you.

6. Step out of your circle, leave the feelings behind. Think of the upcoming situation now … how does it feel knowing you have your 'Bring It On' feelings ready and waiting for you?

Photocopiable:

Teacher's notes

Worksheet 10.3: The upgraded Ferrari (45 minutes)

This worksheet provides an opportunity for students to recognise their progress and formulate some ideas for the future. It is a way of rounding off the work completed and gives them a chance to reflect on where they have come from and where they would like to be. The task is a safe way of self-assessing which also enhances self-esteem. In addition it can be used to bring the programme of work to an end and close the group.

The task involves students drawing around their hands three times on one side of a large piece of paper. On the first hand, to the left of the page, the students need to write statements that will acknowledge any past behaviour, attitudes or feelings they had about themselves, school, home, friends, etc. If this work has been completed as a programme of study they should note what was going on for them at school and home when they started. On the second hand, in the middle of the page, the students must write statements regarding what is going on for them in the present. This should include the things that have changed positively for them. It may also include how they feel about the work ending, especially if it has been completed as a continuous programme. On the third hand, the students should write statements about where they plan to be in five years' time. Once the hands have been completed the students need to connect them all together in some way, putting a padlock on the connection between the second and third hand. By doing this they acknowledge the progress they have made and whilst the first hand is still part of them the padlock reminds them that they need to keep strongly connected to the improvements they have made.

Once they have finished the students need to read out what they have written on their handprints.

These can be rolled up, tied with a ribbon, and presented to all students as if they were degree certificates.

Top tips and common pitfalls

Don't be surprised by their honesty or the accuracy of the assessments they make of themselves when they start on the first/past hand.

Encourage them to acknowledge all of the changes they have made and praise them.

Let them share their progress with the rest of the group.

Allow them to decorate and colour the hand pictures if there is time.

Provide an opportunity, if appropriate, for them to take contact details of other members of the group if this is the last time they will meet.

Let them know how to remain in contact with staff and reassure them that support is there if this is required and appropriate.

The upgraded Ferrari

1. Think of the 'you' that started this work. Draw around your hand and write on to the picture the answers to the following: what did this 'you' believe? Describe that 'you'? How did that 'you' feel about school? Work? The future?

2. Now think about the 'you' you are today. Draw around your hand again and write on to the picture the answers to the following: what does this upgraded 'you' think and feel about school? How have you changed? How do 'you' feel now about the future?

3. As you finish, think about the 'you' in five years' time. Draw around your hand a third time and write on to the picture the answers to the following: what does this 'you' think and feel? What is this 'you' doing?

4. Think about the connection between your handprints. Draw in how these are connected. Make sure that the connection between hands 2 and 3 is very strong and exactly as you want it.

Case study

I use the metaphor for this work as being like a car that has been to the garage for a makeover. It has had its engine cleaned and new alloy wheels put on and as a Ferrari it is now ready for the future. Rob (14) sat next to me completing this task and had written a lot of detail on his printed hands. He had started out being in a lot of trouble both within and outside of school and his second hand clearly acknowledged the progress he had made whilst the third hand listed plans to become a mechanic. As it came to Rob to read his hands out he looked at me and said, 'I know I have done well Chris, but what if I break down next week?' Please take note of Rob's comment and make sure the group has contact details for each other and staff as this is important. He has never needed our support, he just needed to know it was there.

 All photocopiable pages can be found on the CD-ROM accompanying this book.

Appendix 1: Specimen parents' letter

Dear Parent/Guardian

I am writing to confirm the arrangements for the start of the Orchard Programme. Your son/daughter will be starting at 8.45am on May 20th and will continue attending every week on the same day for nine weeks. Uniform does not have to be worn. Your child will be picked up from home by taxi at 8.00am and returned home by taxi when we finish at 1.30pm. If for any reason your child is unable to attend please ring 01772 788584 and let Chris or Andrew know; you will also have to contact your child's school and inform them. Lunch will be provided for the pupils at a cost of £2.00 per day; please ensure that your child has this amount with them each week. If your child has free school meals then this will be automatically taken care of.

We are very excited about the Orchard Programme and have developed a programme of work with the aim of developing the pupils' own self-awareness and giving them both the understanding and strategies to enable them to achieve. The work involves your child setting goals and we would ask you to support us. If you want to call in and have a chat with us about any of this then please do.

We will be having an 'Open Afternoon' during the programme which you are invited to and where you can come and have a look at some of the work we will have done. We will send more details of this nearer the time.

I am looking forward to meeting you and if you have any concerns please do not hesitate to contact us.

Kind regards

Chris Parry-Mitchell, Andrew Swift and John Pilling

Appendix 2: Specimen parents' open afternoon invitation

Dear Parent/Guardian

We would like to invite you to visit the Orchard Programme between 1pm and 2pm on the day your child usually attends, on either Tuesday 6th July, Wednesday 7th July or Thursday 8th July.

We can discuss with you then the plan of work we are completing and how well your son/daughter is progressing whilst also being able to answer any questions you may have. We and the students will be serving you with light refreshments.

Your child will be able to leave with you.

We look forward to meeting you.

Chris Mitchell

Andrew Swift

John Pilling

Appendix 3: Specimen student programme evaluation

Student programme evaluation

1. I have enjoyed the work we have done (rate this out of ten with ten being the best)

2. The most useful things I have learnt here are ...

3. The least useful things that I have learnt here are ...

4. If you had to describe this course to someone else what would you say?

5. Anything else?

Thank you!

Appendix 4: Specimen school referral

Pupil admission form

Please complete all sections and include any other information that you consider relevant. Please email the completed form to office@orchardproject.lancs.sch.uk or send to The Orchard Programme, 30 St Vincents Road, Preston, PR2 8QA (Tel: 01772 788 584).

Many thanks for your co-operation

School:

Pupil Name:

Sex:

Pupil Date of Birth:

Year/Form:

Name of Parent/Carer:

Address:

Telephone:

Mobile:

Emergency Contact Number:

Email address:

Entitled to Free School Meals:

UPN Number:

SEN: School Action –

Attendance % in last term:

Parental permission is requested:

- Is the young person aware of this request and willing to cooperate with the intervention?

    YES/NO (please indicate)

- Are parents/carers positive in supporting this intervention?

    YES/NO (please indicate)

- Has parental consent been given for photographs to be used for display purposes?

    YES/NO (please indicate)

Application completed by:

Contact telephone number/email address:

Please rate each item using the following scale:

1	2	3	4
No cause for concern	Mild cause for concern	Cause for concern	Serious cause for concern

- Arrives late and/or truants from lessons: 1 2 3 4 (please circle appropriate number)

- Comments:

- Is disruptive in lessons: 1 2 3 4

- Comments:

- Ability to remain on task: 1 2 3 4

- Comments:

- Attitude towards other pupils: 1 2 3 4

- Comments:

- Attitude towards members of staff: 1 2 3 4

- Comments:

- Attitude towards other students/young people: 1 2 3 4

- Comments:

- Behaviour in unstructured time: 1 2 3 4

- Comments:

- Displays aggressive tendencies: 1 2 3 4

- Comments:

- Confidence/self-esteem: 1   2   3   4

- Comments:

- Cooperates in group activities: 1 2 3 4

- Comments:

- Has been excluded from school: 1 2 3 4

- Comments:

- What is the student/young person good at/enjoys doing?

- Comments:

- What targets would be appropriate?

1.	
2.	

Appendix 5: Specimen student self-assessment form

Pupil self-assessment form

Name:..

Date of birth:....................................

School:..

How do you feel about school at the moment? (Circle the relevant number.)

The worst it has been					The best it has been
	1	2	3	4	5	

What do you enjoy doing at school and what are you good at?

What do you enjoy doing in your spare time?

What are the main difficulties you are having?

Have you ever been excluded from school?

How does the following apply to you?	Always	Quite often	Sometimes	Never	Details?
I can talk about how I feel					
I can accept feedback without feeling angry					
I can listen to other people's opinions					
I can control my temper					
I can explain my opinion clearly					
I can make my own decisions					
I can relax					

Do you go to all your lessons and arrive on time? What happens?

Do you find it easy to get on with other people? What happens?

What makes you angry? What happens?

What would you like to improve on in school?

-

-

-

Have you had any help from anyone else about the difficulties you have had?

At the end of the programme, when things have improved for you, how will you feel?

What will you see?

What will you hear others saying and what will you be saying to yourself?

Appendix 6: Specimen student's letter

Dear

Your nine-week Orchard programme begins on September <>.

When you arrive at the Centre at 8.45 am you will be met by Chris and Andrew who will be working with you throughout the course.

Each week will follow a similar pattern of learning sessions with regular breaks. We will be covering different topics each week and the first session is called 'TOP United' where we will all be getting to know each other and looking at the programme content. When you have worked successfully all morning you will have some free time and lunch before you are collected at 1.30pm.

If you have any questions then please call us on 01772 788584.

We are looking forward to seeing you there.

Regards

Chris and Andrew

Appendix 7: Specimen brochure

Results

The 'KNOW HOW' at the Orchard programme has been delivered to over 120 students. Attendance for each of the cohorts has been excellent. Students complete a PASS questionnaire on entry and exit which has enabled us (and them) to see any significant improvements. In 99% of the group their PASS results showed improvements in all of the areas questioned. The largest improvements in relation to the PASS have been in (a) confidence in learning, (b) preparedness for learning, (c) perceived learning capacity, and (d) self-regard as a learner; all of these are vital if young people are to succeed.

Following the completion of the programme the students are supported back in their school settings via one-to-one sessions, group sessions and in lessons as needed.

Comments from students

'I've been given an award for the most improved student out of all the school and the head teacher wanted to shake my hand … wicked'. (DM)

'If you want to change then you have to do this; it's down to you'. (JC)

'It's like a normal class but more fun and more useful, you've helped me!!' (PG)

Chris Mitchell and Andrew Swift

Chris is an experienced teacher and manager who has worked extensively in schools. She delivers INSET training to staff around Engagement and Behaviour Management. Andrew is an experienced HLTA who is also currently completing a degree in 'Positive Practice with Young People'.

30 St Vincents Road,   Preston, PR2 3QA   Tel: 01772 788 584

office@orchardproject.lancs.sch.uk

The Orchard Programme

Guide for Schools and Parents/Carers

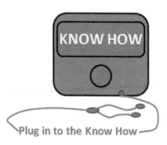

The 'Know How'

The 'Know How' Programme at the Orchard is a psycho-educational programme designed to 'enable' those young people at risk within the school setting by teaching them how to think, communicate, behave and relate to one another and other people in more useful ways.

The programme will benefit the students by enabling them to understand and manage their own emotional state better, develop their self-esteem and raise their aspirations; to better understand their own learning preferences and become self-directed learners; and to allow them to engage better with others and reduce conflict. It is designed to assist young people to think, communicate, act and relate to each other in ways that are more personally and socially useful.

The programme has been designed using a range of well-established frameworks including Neuro Linguistic Programming (NLP), Transactional Analysis (TA), Learning Theories, Solution Focused Coaching and Humanistic Psychology. The 'KNOW HOW' Programme translates some of the most useful aspects of these approaches into child-friendly language, activities and techniques.

How is it Delivered?

The programme is taught to young people in a small group setting over a nine-week period. The day is structured around three sessions where different but related topics are discussed and worked on as a group through a series of specific worksheets. The pupils are encouraged to share their experiences and provide each other with support and assistance.

What the programme includes

- Models for understanding the behaviours of ourselves and others.

- Emotional state management techniques.

- Communication and rapport skills.

- Self-esteem and aspiration.

Bibliography, further reading, websites and training courses

Further reading

This is not an exhaustive list of books: some will provide more in-depth knowledge and will allow you to read around a topic while others marked with a * are of a more practical nature.

Austin, A. (2007) *The Rainbow Machine: Tales from a Neurolinguist's Journal*, Boulder, CO: Real People Press.

Bandler, R. (1985) *Using Your Brain for a Change*, Moab, UT: Real People Press.

Bandler, R. and Grinder, J. (1975) *The Structure of Magic I: A Book about Language and Therapy*, Palo Alto, CA: Science and Behaviour Books.

Bandler, R. and Grinder, J. (1979) *Frogs into Princes*, Moab, UT: Real People Press.

Beever, S. (2009) *Happy Kids Happy You: Using NLP to Bring out the Best in Ourselves and the Children We Care For*, Camarthen, UK: Crown House Publishing Ltd.

*Berne, E. (1964) *Games People Play*, New York: Grove Press.

Dilts, R. (1990) *Changing Belief Systems with NLP*, Capitola, CA: Metapublications.

Dilts, R., Grinder, J., Bandler, R., Delozier, J. (1980) *Neuro-Linguistic Programming: The Study of Subjective Experience*, Cupertino, CA: Meta Publications.

*Freed, A. (1976) *TA for Teens*, Rolling Hills Estates, CA: Jalmar Press Inc.

*Freed, A. and Freed, M. (1971) *TA for Kids*, Rolling Hills Estates, CA: Jalmar Press Inc.

Grove, D. J. and Panzer, B. I. (1989) *Resolving Traumatic Memories – Metaphors and Symbols in Psychotherapy*, New York: Irvington.

Hall, M. (2000) *Meta-States*, Revised Edition, Grand Junction, CO: ET Publications.

*Harland, P. (2009) *The Power of Six: A Six Part Guide to Self Knowledge*, London: Wayfinder Press.

*Harland, P. (2011) *Trust Me I am the Patient: Clean Language, Metaphor and the New Psychology of Change*, London: Wayfinder Press

Jensen, E. (2008) *Brain Based Learning: The New Paradigm of Teaching*, 2nd edition, London, UK: Sage Publications Ltd.

Karpman, S. (1968) 'Fairy tales and script dramas', *Transactional Analysis*, 7(26): 39–43.

Kolb, D. A. (1984) *Experiential Learning: Experience as the Source of Learning and Development*, Englewood Cliffs, NJ: Prentice Hall.

Lawley, J. D. and Tompkins, P.L. (2000) *Metaphors in Mind: Transformation through Systemic Modelling*, London, UK: The Developing Company Press.

Locke, E. A. (1968) 'Toward a theory of task motivation and incentives', *Organizational Behaviour and Human Performance*, 3(2): 157–89.

MacLean, P. D. (1990) *The Triune Brain in Evolution: Role in Paleocerebral Functions*, New York: Plenum Press.

Maslow, A. H. (1987) *Motivation and Personality*, Hong Kong: Longman Asia Ltd.

Mehrabian, A. (1972) *Nonverbal Communication*, Chicago, IL: Aldine-Atherton.

*O'Connor, J. (2001) *NLP Workbook: A Practical Guide to Achieving the Results You Want*, London, UK: Thorsons.

*Owen, N. (2001) *The Magic of Metaphor*, Carmarthen, UK: Crown House Publishing Ltd.

*Quilliam, S. (2003) *What Makes People Tick?* London, UK: Element, Harper Collins Publishers Ltd.

*Steiner, C. (1977) *The Original Warm Fuzzy Tale*, Sacramento, CA: Jalamar Press Inc.

Stewart, A. and Joines, V. (2002) *TA Today: A New Introduction to Transactional Analysis*, Nottingham and Chapel Hill: Lifespace Publishing.

Walker, C. (1997) *Training Attention Ltd: Systems Thinking in Practice* [Online]. Available at www.trainingattention.co.uk (accessed April 2012).

Websites and training courses

- www.nlp4education.co.uk is a subdivision of the Instit2te of NLP for public service. It provides information as to available courses particular to the delivery and content of this book and also has information about short education-specific courses and training. Contact the author on info@nlp4publicservice.co.uk

- www.instit2uteofnlpforpublicservice provides information about the practical and applied use of NLP for those involved in delivering public service. The Instit2te supplies recognised NLP training, consultancy, facilitation and research in an applied way that makes a real difference to clients, students, workers, managers and organisations. The service is provided in a way that is consistent with public service values, by people who are skilled in NLP and experienced in public service. Email info@nlp4publicservice.co.uk

- Reaching Hard to Reach Families offers information and psycho-educational workshops and strategies for professionals working with families, their children and teenagers. Email info@reachingfamilies.co.uk

- Clean Language: www.cleanlanguage.co.uk provides information on clean language, systemic modelling and the work of David Grove

- Magical Spelling: www.magicalspellinglimited.com contains information on the Magical Spelling® process, training, accredited trainers and the JMU research.

- Creating Learning Systems: www.trainingattention.co.uk contains information on inspiring capability in young people so they become experts on themselves and facilitators for one another.

- The Spelling Strategy: www.nlpuniversitypress.com contains information as regards Robert Dilt's research and strategies.

- ITAA: www.itaa-net.org provides information about training organisations for Transactional Analysis.